Instant Patwa

Speak and Understand Jamaican Patois

© Copyright 2020 by A. Henriques. All rights reserved. Published in the U.S.A. This book may not, in part or in whole, be reproduced or distributed in any form or medium without the author's prior written permission.

Written by a native speaker, this book shares the author's skill in the *listening comprehension* and *pronunciation* of Jamaican Patois (Patwa) relative to English. The author is not liable for any loss associated with this book. As expected, learning is a function not only of material and instruction, but also of students' efforts and inclination. This book teaches only spoken Patwa. The written Patwa you pick up from this book is coincidental.

Instead of the Foreword
IV

Starting Right
V

How to Use This Book
VII

PAAT WAN
1

The Top 20 Patwa Traits and Accent Nuances
2

My Patwalfabet
4

English Digraphs and Blends as Compared to Patwa
6

Jumiekan Patwa in Akshan! (Jamaican Patwa in Action!)
10

Conversation/Useful Phrases
13

PAAT TUU
15

Prefix and Suffix Patterns
16

Frequent Elision: How the Words "Run Together"
21

Parts of Speech
25

Articles
25

Personal Pronouns
27

PAAT TRII
32

Verbs
33

Present Tense
36

The Negative
47

PAAT FWOR
50

False Cognates
51

Idioms
60

Lifesaver on the Road
69

Rasta Patwa
73

PAAT FAIV
75

Patwa-English Vocabulary
76

English-Patwa Vocabulary
101

Cognate Lists
109

Instead of the Foreword

The Top Five Things That Make It Simple to Learn Patwa

1. Number

   We have the option of putting the word *dem* after the noun in the plural. "Man" is mostly the same in English and Patwa, but the plural "men" is either *"man"* or *"man dem"* in Patwa. ("Man" is also a frequent filler, often genderless as in "friend.")

2. Conjugation

   There are no verb endings. Verbs are stems, not varying with person.

3. Tense

   Verbs don't change in the simple past tense, but we can add the word *did*: *Mi si.* (I see/saw.) *Mi did si.* (I saw.) The future adds *wi, gwain*, or *aggo*: *Mi wi si.* (I will see.) Present continuous puts *"a"* and past continuous adds *"did"* to the *"a"* before the verb: *Mi a goh.* (I am going.) *Mi dida goh.* (I was going.)

4. Gender

   In Patwa, only people (and pets or livestock, if referred to as male or female) have gender; inanimate objects do not. Articles, adjectives, etc., are neutral.

5. Vocabulary

   Patwa has plenty of English loanwords. This book lists many of them. It's that simple.

Starting Right

Jamrak, Jumieka, J.A., Yaad -- call her what you will! Sweet Jamaica, 146 miles long and 51 miles at widest, is an irresistible country. English is the national language, but the popular tongue of the island's near three million people[1] is Patwa (Jamaican Creole), which is a mixture of the masses' ancestral African languages and colonial-era English.[2] Patwa's earthiness is all African. Broken English is this: *Wat yu want?* (What do you want?) *Weer yu goin'?* (Where are you going?) Asking the same two questions in pure Patwa takes different skill: *Weh yu waaŋ? Weh yaago?* (Also spelt: *"We yaago?"* This book adds "h" to the Patwa *"we"* to prevent confusion with the English first-person plural.)

    Written Patwa was always subjectively anglicized due to the absence of a standard written form: *"giez"* got misspelt "g-a -z -e" because it means "gaze" in English. Fortunately, the Cassidy/JLU Orthography[3] now provides a written standard. Whenever this book uses non-standard shortcuts for quick fluency in spoken Patwa, we aim to put some standard spelling in parentheses. For instance, when we keep the English hard "i" + silent ending "e" in words that sound the same in Patwa, we'll have the standard spelling in parentheses and a diaresis ï in Patwa aï to distinguish it from English "ai": "time" *(taïm)*, "line" *(laïn)* — also "igh": "light" *(laït)*, "right" (raït). Unlike English and French spelling, Patwa spelling has no silent letters. English "ai" is *ie* in Patwa. Patwa *"kliem"* means "claim" in English; *"f-r-i-e-d"* (fried pronounced "fr -- *yed*" rhyming with "Fred") is

---

[1] The World Factbook, July 2020

[2] *Jamaica Talk: Three Hundred Years of the English language in Jamaica*, F.G. Cassidy (University Press of the West Indies, 1961)

[3] The Jamaican Language Unit, the Department of Language, Linguistics and Philosophy, UWI, Mona.

Patwa for "afraid" and not English "fried" as in "fried fish." The English "-ed" past tense structure isn't in Patwa, as you see: *"Mi frai tuu plaantn."* ("I fried two plantains.") Though not a writing text, this book observes simple Patwa phonics: The word "bough" sounds the same in Patwa, but the Patwa spelling *(b-o-u)* has one pronunciation, whereas English "ough" has many (e.g., "though that bough of thought runs through a trough").

Instant Patwa names and simplifies "Patlish": a Jamaican sociolect used by some Jamaicans who view Patwa as low-register Pidgin English. Patlish speakers try not to stray far from English (their perceived lexifier) as they speak Patwa. They fear Patwa will hinder their social mobility.[4] That's a valid concern in Jamaica. When you hear *"ah"* instead of *"mi"* (meaning "I"), or *"dwoh"* instead of *"noh"* (meaning "don't") you're hearing Patlish **or** (conversely) an up-market variant. It is my dearest desire that this book will be a lifeboat for the people who are drowning in Patlish and whose mastery of English is being hampered by the lack of an ESL approach that builds them a bridge over deep language differences.

Remember, Patwa has a Jamaican accent, but the Jamaican accent is not only used for Patwa. Naturally, it's used (to varying degrees) when Jamaicans speak English -- they're Jamaican. A French accent doesn't necessarily mean someone is speaking French. Remembering that simple fact lets you see why some "Patwa" seems easier to understand than others. What might sound like Patwa could actually be English. At any rate, after reading this book, you can sound as Jamaican as you like and *understand* Patwa. This is dedicated to everyone who loves Patwa! It's an unorthodox shortcut to real Patwa. Are you ready? *Mek wi staat!* (Let's begin!)

---

[4] For a keen understanding of language's link to social mobility in any society, read Basil Bernstein's classic *Class, Codes and Control* (Routledge & Kegan Paul, Ltd., 2003), and *Language, Race and the Global Jamaican*, First Edition (Palgrave MacMillan, 2020) by Dr. H. Devonish and Dr. K. Carpenter.

How to Use This Book

- This is your guide, a must-have phrasebook of idioms and everyday Patwa. Your key to comprehension, it does what it says: It gives you instant Patwa. Take it with you on every vacation – the book itself is a vacation!

- Literal spelling does *not* denote emphasis. Practice aloud without over-enunciating. Patwa sounds mellow, because no syllable is overstressed.

- *Instant Patwa* takes the layman's approach to pronunciation, by primarily using not diacriticals but examples of English words that rhyme with Patwa words.

- Refer often to "The Top 20 Patwa Traits and Accent Nuances" and "My Patwalfabet" to make Patwa pronunciation natural and intuitive to you.

- "Regional" in this book refers to rural/parochial speech and tells you what you'll *hear*, **not** how to speak. Many urban/suburban Jamaicans don't know rural Patwa, but rural speakers understand other Jamaicans' speech.

- Other than standalone "I" and loanwords like *"flu"* and *"oh,"* each vowel has a short sound. To remind you of that, this book puts "h" at the end of *"we"* (*weh*, meaning "what" or "where") and *"go"* (*goh*) and replaces *u* with *w* in *uol*: *wol* (hold, whole).

- Patwa *"de"* is pronounced *deh*. *"De"* **isn't** "the" as in broken English. It's an adverb and a locative verb: *Yu de de?* "Are you there?" (This book adds an "h" to Patwa words such as *de* and *no* to remind you, from time to time, that *de* has the short "e" and no has the short "o" sound: *Yu deh deh?*) *Mi noh de weh dem de.* I'm not where they are (this could be literal or figurative). *A de-so mi de:* "That's where I am."

- *Instant Patwa* doubles consonants: Patwa *piis* (English "peace" or "piece") might be p-e-e-s-s, in this book, to show you our *s* is **not** a "z" sound. This book gradually drops the anglicized "ee" and replaces it with the Patwa *"ii"* (when you've acclimatized enough).

- Double-vowels are long. *aa* is "aah"; *ii* and *uu* are English *ee* and long *oo*. Note, *ie* is "ye" as in "yes." Patwa's *ai* is a *hard i. For instance, tchraiangl* is "triangle". The "t" in front of *chraiangl* is to remind you of the Patwa "ch" as in English "cheese"/*chiiz*.

- Use this book's "Pieces of Immersion" to immerse yourself in Patwa fun!

PAAT WAN

(Part One)

The Top 20 Patwa Traits and Accent Nuances

1. *"Man":* a legendary Patwa filler with a short *a* as in *polka*. It is the last syllable of "ottoman." This "man" is genderless, like "friend."

2. Plenty of fillers: *a, aam, ee, e-yer, noh, yaa, issi,* and *innoh/ino*. The most common one *"a"* can mean many things, including "there is."

3. The long hard English "a" becomes soft "i" + short soft "e": "play" is *plieh*; "claim" is *kliem;* "date" is *diet* (rhymes with "immediate").

4. No st/sp/nd endings   only "s" or "n": fast/*faas*, lisp/*liss,* end/*en*.

5. The English "or" ending is *o* or *a* (e.g., mirror/*mirro*). Inner "ir" becomes *o* (or *u* in this book: dirty shirt/*doti shut*), birth/*birt;* firm/*firm*.

6. "-Urst" or "-irst" becomes *os* in standard written Patwa and *us* in this book (e.g., first/*fos*, burst/*bus*). However, "surf" keeps its "r" just like: *servant; verss; permishan*/permission. "Work"is *wok,* and *werk* is a variant of *wok*.

7. For some short words, vowel endings, are short, yet *tree* is a long *e*.

8. English "ar/or" preceding a consonant is *aa* (e.g., part/*paat;* organ/*aagan;* argue/*aagiu*). Preceding a vowel, it's *ar* (e.g., arrange/*arienj*).

9. The English prefix "re-" is often the Patwa suffix *bak*, so "restart" is *staat bak*: "Turn off the truck, and restart it." *Tun aaf di chok, an staat it bak.* However, English "react" is Patwa *riak*. ("Act" is *ak*.)

10. Velar ŋ (like "n" in "song") is the sound at the end of *waa, kian, kiaa* and *ee* ("want, can, can't and eh"). *Waan* is "warn"; *waa(ŋ)* is want.

11. The "-tion" English ending is *-shan* in Patwa (e.g., action = *akshan*).

12. English "s" *(zh)* in "usual//vision," etc., is Patwa *j:* "vision"/*vijan*.

13. "H" often disappears (e.g., "behave"/*biev*; but *"ch"* is prevalent (e.g., "true"/*chuu;* "through"/*chuu;* regionally *"stupid"*/*chupid*, etc.).

14. Patwa repeats some verbs and adjectives for emphasis and/or to suggest that an action is done repeatedly. For example, if we want to say, "They are calling repeatedly," we would say, *"Dem a kaal kaal."* To say, "It's very new," we would say, *"It niuu niuu."*

15. No English "oi" digraph: "voice" sounds like English "vice" in Patwa and is spelt *vaïs*. "Boiled" is Patwa *bwaïl* (which rhymes with English "style").

16. The starting English "du" is often Patwa *"j"*: duty/*juuty*; duco/*juuco*.

17. The "ve'" in "give" is often dropped.

18. English participles (-ing) are only Patwa adjectives (e.g., *a grinnin dizaasta*/a grinning disaster). Note: They are grinning. = *Dem a grin.* The Patwa version of English "-ed" words are adjectives **or** are actual verb stems (e.g., "exhausted": *Im aggo exaastid dem.* He's going to exhaust them.)

19. The "-own" and "-und" in "down" and in the noun "ground" become *ng*: *dung, grung/grong*. Note: "around" is *rong,* but "round" (shape) is *roun* and sound is *soun*. Re *"rong"*: Patwa "o" is **only** the "o" in English "son."

20. Word endings often link to the beginnings of words that follow. Let's call this elision "The Patwa Liaison." For example, *kian goh* ("can go") is *kiangoh*. (*Kiangoh* rhymes with tango, the Spanish dance.) Also, Patwa often drops the "d" from *"did"* so that *"did"* becomes *"id."* *"Dem did goh; im did stieh,"* can be: *"Dem id goh; im id stieh."* ("They went; he stayed.").

My Patwalfabet

Created for this book, *My Patwalfabet* won't be strange to users of the International Phonetic Alphabet. *My Patwalfabet* differs from the English alphabet. As you read Patwa words, remember, single Patwa vowels are short. If you hear an English vowel's name in a Patwa word, it's spelt out or double (e.g., *yuunit*/unit, *sii*/sea), but Rasta "*I*" says its name.

a = short *a* as in polka. (English hard "a" becomes *ie*: "ye-" as in *yes*)

aa = aah (one long, smooth, open sound)

ai = long i, as in English "kite" (*Mi a trai mi be*s: I'm trying my best.)

b = same as English

c = pronounced as English "k"

ch = always as in English "cheese"

d = same as English (but often omitted at the start of the Patwa *"did"*)

e = always soft, as in *pet*; "er" is sometimes pronounced as in English

f = same as English

g = hard g (e.g., game/*giem*; gas/*gias*: gamble/*giambl;* glass/*glaas;* glad/*glad*)

h = no starting "h"; *sh* digraph same as English. Patwa *ch* **isn't** "k."

i = same as English soft "i" (e.g., "pin"), but it stays separate in ai *(aï)*

ii = ē like English "ee" (This book uses *ii* but also uses English "ee.")

j, k, l, m, n = same as English; "nk" and some "ng" (tank, sing) = same as English

o = as in English "son"; English "but" is Patwa *bot.* (English ō is Patwa *uo.*)

ou = as in the English "out" (Patwa *lou* is the second syllable of "allow.")

p = same as English

q = not in Patwa (English "qu" = Patwa *kw*)

r = same as English, less ending rhoticity (except *wier*/wear, *klier*/clear, *karier*/career, etc.)

s = mostly same as English, but Patwa "s" is not a "z" sound

sh = same as in English

t = This is the same as English but that there's no "th" and no ending *t* after *s*.

u = *u* as in the English word "push"

uo = *woh: Nuo* is "know" in English, but because *"nuo"* looks like the English loanword "duo" we avoid dissonance by spelling *nuo* "n-w-o-h" or *"n-u-o-h"* in this book, to remind you that Patwa *uo* is only **one** syllable.)

uu = sounds like the **long** English "oo"

v = same as English (Regionally, a "v" sounds like a "b" as in Spanish.)

w, x, y = same as English, but *x* is never a *z* sound (alternative spelling: *ks*)

z = same as English, but that there's no *zh* sound in Patwa (only *j* instead)

Note: The Cassidy/Jamaican Language Unit (CJLU) Orthography[5]

Vowels: **a**/*apl* (apple), **e**/*en* (end), **i**/*ink*, **o**/*bota* (butter), **u**/*kuk* (cook)

Double Vowels: aa/*baat* (bath), ii/*diip* (deep), uu/*Fuud inkluud.* (Food is included.)

Diph.: ie/*kriet* (create), uo/*uots* (oats), aï/*daï* (high/die), ou/*kou* (how/cow)

---

[5] The CJLU Orthography's standard Patwa is on the Jamaican Language Unit's social media (YouTube).

English Digraphs and Blends as Compared to Patwa

Let's reinforce and add to what we've just covered in "My Patwalfabet":

If *oa* or *ou* is a long *o*, Patwa makes it *uo*: "Load" is *luod*. "Soul" is *suol*.

The Patwa *"uu"* is like the English long "oo" in boot/*buut,* food/*fuud*. When Patwa *tuu* ("too") means "excessively" and precedes any adjective but **"much"** it's a long sound; when it means "also" or ends a statement, it's short. Example: *Dem **tuu** faass (faas); dem chat **tu** much – im du dat **tu**.* ("They're too nosy; they talk too much – he does that, too.")

English **ending** "-er" becomes "*a*": hammer = *amma*. However, please note inner "er": "verb" is *verb* – the middle "er" remains, exactly as in English.

The English "aw" or "au" sound is Patwa *aa*: "Dancehall" is *daansaal*. The word "drama" sounds the same as English but is spelt *d-r-a-a-m-a*.

English "-tle" can become *-kl* (gentle = *jenkl*; little = *likl*).

There is no *zhu* pronunciation as in the English word "casual" (Patwa: *kajual*). There is only *j* in words whose English version has a "-sion" ending or a "-usu-" or "-sur-" combination (e.g., version/*verjan;* usual/*yuujwal;* measure/*meja*). "*Get wan ruula an meja it:* Get a ruler and measure it."

English "th" is not in Patwa: "that/ *dat;* them/*dem;* thanks/*tanks;* "with": *wid*.

English "-dle" is *-gl* in Patwa: "riddle" is *rigl* (sounds like English "wriggle"); "middle" is *migl;* cuddle is *cugl* (rhymes with "snuggle"); handle is *angl*.

As you move forward, don't hesitate to refer to this part of the book as needed.

Patwa in Akshan: Recognizing Popular Lines

These lines show the phonics you just learnt, as well as a preview of articles and the future tense.

Movie Lines

1. A Few Good Men   *"Yu waa di chuut? Yu kiaa **angl** di chuut!"*
2. Field of Dreams   *"If yu bil it, im wi kom."*
3. Shaft (Theme)   *"Im a wan komplikietid man."*
4. The Terminator   *"Mi wi kom bak."* (Here, *kom* suggests "be.")
5. The Godfather   *"Mi aggo mek im a aafa im kiaa rifiuuz."*
6. Scarface   *"Se elluo tu mi likl fren."*
7. Taxi Driver   *"A mi yaa taak? A **mi** yaa taak?"*

1. "You want the truth? You can't handle the truth." (Nicholson)
2. "If you build it, he will come." (Whisperer to Costner)
3. "He's a complicated man." (Hayes) Patwa *"im"* means "him" and "he."
4. "I'll be back." (Schwarzenegger)
5. "I'm gonna make him an offer he can't refuse." (Brando)
6. "Say hello to my little friend." (Pacino)
7. "You talkin' a me? You talkin' a me?" (de Niro)

Lines of Poetry & Prayers

Shiekspier an di Gaspl inna Patwa (Shakespeare and the Gospel in Patois)

1. Hamlet: *Fi bi, aar noh fi bi? A dat a di kwestian.* (To be or not to be?)

2. Iscariot: *A mii, Laad?* (Is it I, Lord? [*Mii* has a long *e* sound: *mee*.]) The reverse is the skeptical disciple asking, *"A yuu, Laad?"*

3. E.B.B.: *Ou mi lov yu? Mek mi count di wie dem!* ("How do I love thee?")

4. Jesus: *Gwaan, an noh sin noh muor.* ("Go forth, and sin no more.")

5. Prayer: *Jeezas, fren tu likl pikni, bih a fren tu mi.* ("Jesus, friend of little children, be a friend to me.") *"Fren tu"* suggests "friend of" **only here**.

Phrases You'll Recognize

Appi Niuu Ier!   Happy New Year!

Merry Krismos! Merry Christmas!

Appi Indipendenss Dieh! Happy Independence Day! (Here, the Patwa word for "day" has "h" at the end (*dieh*), whereas in standard spelling it would have no *h*. Patwa *"die"* (day) rhymes with English "yeah.")

Dive in! Try your hand at translating this Patwa passage, before reading the translation below it:

Filla eena Patwa

Yu wi si "yaa" regiula inna da buk ya. It de a di en a nuff friez, inna infaamal kanva-sieshan, espeshali inna di imperitiv. Noh badda wanda tuu aad bout it. It kian kuox smadi, aar it kian sojess "yu ier" (fi ri-infuos sopm). Apaat fram dat, it noh tuu meen notn. Yu naa goh si "yaa" az a filla inna kwestian. Yu wi si "a" in front a evriting.

English Translation:
Fillers in Patwa
You will see *"yaa"* regularly in this book. It's at the end of many phrases in informal conversation, especially in the imperative. Don't bother to wonder too hard about it. It can coax somebody or can suggest "you hear" (to reinforce something). Apart from that, it doesn't much mean anything. You won't see *"yaa"* as a filler in any question. You'll see *"a"* in front of almost everything.

Did you translate most of it on your own? *Kangratiulieshan!* (Congratulations!)

Memba Dis! (Remember This!)
Reinforcing "ie" and Introducing "ia"

Brogue meets Patwa: Among the people brought to labor on colonial plantations in Jamaica were the Irish, who added their own lovely flavor to Patwa. Even caricatures of an Irish accent sound like Patwa. If you've ever seen the movie Shrek, you've heard the "i" that sounds like the English "y" in the word "yes." It's similar to the "i" in the English word "resilient." That "yeh" is the sound of the Patwa *ie,* which always replaces the English hard *a* (the "a" that says its name). The letter "a" doesn't say its name in Patwa. English "name" is Patwa *niem* (ñem). "Play" is *plie*; "care" is *kier*. That's the **only** "ie" sound in Patwa.

That "i" that sounds like "y" not only helps to replace hard "a"; it also precedes the **soft** "a" that follows "**c**" or "**g**" (e.g., cab/*kiab*; cabbage/*kiabbij*; camp/*kiamp*; can/*kiaŋ*; car/*kiar*; cast/*kiaass*; cat/*kiat*; garbage/*giaabij;* guard/ *giaad*; gas/*gias;* etc.). However, English "calm" is Patwa *kaam* and "garage" is *goraaj*. **Also,** Mistake is *mistiek,* but "take" is ***tek***, and "make" is ***mek***.

The *"ya"* sound does **not** follow other consonants: band/*ban*; darker/ *daaka*; nap/*nap*, pastor/*paasta*; rag/*rag*; vault/*vaalt*; talk/*taak*; walk/ *waak,* wall/ *waal,* etc. By the way, "dam" is *dam*, and "damp" is *damp*, but damn is *diam*. Note that the "ya" does **not** apply to "co" words, though some sound like *can*: *kantruol*/control, *kanvasieshan/* conversation.

Sometimes you won't hear "ya" in names. Camille, Karyn, Carla, Carol and Carlene, would be *Kameel, Karin, Kaala, Karal* and *Kaaleen.* However, Cathy, Kate, Gary and Gabriel would be *Kiatty, Kiet, Giery/ Giary* and *Giebriel*. Let's have some fun with names in the next exercise!

Pieces of Immersion: Hear Your Name in Patwa

Jumiekan Patwa in Akshan! (Jamaican Patwa in Action!)
Names like Sean, Steve, Lisa, Kermit and Ralph sound the same in Patwa as in English. How does your name sound in Patwa?

If your name is…	*Your name sounds like…*
Abby/Abigail/Adam	*Abby/Abigiel (A-big-yell)/Adam*
Alan/Ali/Allen/Adelaide	*Alan/Ali/Allen/Adiliehd (A-dill-yed)*
Amanda/Amy/Angela	*Amanda/Yeh-mi (iemi)/Anjela*
Andrew/Anthony/Arthur	*Anju/Antunny/Aata*
Aaron/Aisha/Asher	*Yieran/A-yeesha/Asha*
Agatha/Ashley/Ashton	*Ag-yatta/Ashli/Ashtan*
Ben/Beth/Billy/Blake	*Ben/Bet/Billy/Bliek*
Candy/Cole/Colette/Curtis	*Kiandy/Kwol/Ka-let/Curtis*
Cameron/Christine/Christopher	*Kiamaran/Kristeen/Kris-tiffa*
Darla/Daryl/Dave/Dennis	*Daala/Da-rell/Diev/Dennis*
Elton/Eric/Erica/Ethan/Evelyn	*El-tan/Eric/Erica/Eetan/Evlin*
Frank/Fred/Frederick	*Frank/Fred/Frejrik*
Garth/Gary/Gene/Gina/Gregory	*Giaat/Giery/Jeen/Jeena/Gregri*
Henry/Hilary/Howard/Horace	*Enry/Illary/Owwad/Arriess*
Idris/Isaac/Ivan/Ivy	*Idris* or *Eedris/I-zik/I-van/I-vi*
Jack/James/Jennifer/John/Joe/Judith	*Jack/Jiemz/Jenifa/Jan/Jwo/Judit*
Kayla/Katherine/Keesha/Keith	*Kiela/Kiatchrin/Keesha/Keet*
Kelly/Ken/Kimberly	*Kelly/Ken/Kimba-li*

Lamar/Laura/Lauren	*Lamaar/Laara/Larren*
Lashawn/Len/Lewis/Liam	*Lashaan/Len/Luuiss/Liam*
Linda/Lorraine/Lucas	*Linda/Larien (Lar-yen)/Lucas*
Mark/Michelle/Michael	*Maak/Michelle/My kal*
Nadine/Natalie/Natasha/Nia	*Na-deen/Natta-lee/Natasha/Nia*
Nikki/Noel/Nora/Norman	*Nikki/Nowell/Nwora/Naa-man*
Paula/Pablo/Patricia/Peter	*Paala/Pablo/Patchreesha/Peeta*
Rachel/Reggie/Regina/Rita	*Rietchel/Reji/Rejina/Ritta* or *Reeta*
Robert/Roger/Rohan/Ryan	*Rabbert/Raja/Rwaan/Ra-yan*
Samuel/Samantha/Sharon	*Sam-yuwell/Samanta/Sherran*
Sierra/Sonia/Shauna/Stacy	*Sierra/Swonia/Shaana/Stiessy*
Tamara/Tara/Tanya/Ted	*Tamaara/Taara/Tanya/Ted*
Thomas/Theodore/Tia/Tina	*Tammass/Tio-dwor/Tia/Teena*
Tom/Trevor/Trish/Tyler	*Taam/Trevva/Trish/Tyla*
Vanessa/Valerie/Vaughn	*Vanessa/Valrih/Vaan*
Veronica/Victor/Vivienne	*Vernica/Vikta/Vivveen*
Vic/Vicki/Victoria/Violet	*Vik/Vikki/Viktworia/Vylet*
Walter/Wanda/Warren/Wendy	*Waalta/Wan-da/Wa-Ren/Wendy*
Wesley/Weston/Will/Wilson	*Wesly [Wezly]/Westan/Will/Wilsn*
Yanique/Yara/Yolanda	*Yaneek/Yaara/Yu-landa*
Zachariah/Zack/Zaire/Zara	*Zaka ra-ya/Zak/Za-yehr/Zaara*

Pronunciation in the above list **isn't** written with all of the new orthography's Patwa phonics. Where Patwa names begin with "i" we use a small "i" **here** to remind you the "i" doesn't say its name; it's short as in *bit* (*e.g., nat wan bit:* "not a bit").

Test Your Skill! *(Tes Yu Skill!)*

Unscramble the letters beside the spaces to find the translation, and fill in the spaces. (Answers are at the bottom of this page.)

Patwa	English
biess (bies)	(sabe)
fiess (fies)	(cafe)
riet	(reta)
rienj	(arneg)
fiem	(emfa)
pliet	(pelat)
niempliet	(enampelat)
kanva sieshan	(ncoversonait)
stiet	(testa)
briev	(breva)
ennywie (enywie)	(nyawya)
giambl	(magble)
kantruol	(ncorolt)
Yu nuoh di wie? <u>You know</u> ?	(hte ywa)

Answer: base, face, rate, range, fame, plate, nameplate, conversation; state, brave, anyway, gamble; control. You know the

Conversation/Useful Phrases

Getting Acquainted

Mi niem Rich. Weh yu niem? (My name's Rich. What's yours?)

Mi niem Kim. Weh yu kom fram? (My name is Kim. Where are you from?)

Wi kom fram di US, mi an mi son dem. (We come from the US, my sons and I.)

Dem a omoch? A omoch a dem? (How old are they? How many of them?)

Kom meet dem. Dem de uova de soh. (Come meet them. They're over there.)

Tipikal Kanvasieshan (Typical Conversation)

Waapm man? It look like wedda. (It luk laïk weda.)
(What's up? It looks like it's out to be rough weather.)

*Weh yu se? Waddat meen? (What did you say? What does that mean?)

It noh meen notn. (It doesn't mean anything.)

Mi waa nuoh. (I want to know.)

It out fi tun inna staam aar orikien. (It's about to turn into a storm/hurricane.)

Oh, an mi didda plan fi goh swim. (Oh? And I was planning to go swimming.)

Memba mi tel yu: stie pan lan; sii rof. (Remember I told you: stay on land;

seas are rough.)

Mi wi goh mi jerk restaraant insted. (I'll go to my jerk restaurant instead.)

Weh dat de? (A dat) mi waa nuo. (Where's that? [That's what] I want to know.)

Kom wi goh. (Let's go.)

*Note the difference between *"Weh yu se?"* (What did you say?) and *"Weh y'a se?"* (What are you saying?), a brotherly greeting meaning "What's up?"

Memba Dis! Kulcha Tip [Remember This! Culture Tip]

Jamaicans grow up hearing this adage: *Mannaz tek yu chuu di werl.* ("Manners take you through the world.") If you neglect "good morning" and "thank you," you might be asked, *"Yu naav noh mannaz?"* ("Don't you have any manners?") Don't give the impression that *"yu naav noh mannaz."* ("You have no manners.") Patwa courtesy words are very similar to their English counterparts. "Please" sounds the same in Patwa (*pliiz*) as in English; so do "welcome" (*welkom*), excuse *(exkiuuz* or *eskiuuz),* and "good night" *(gud naït).* "Pardon" is *paadn*; "thanks" is *tanks.*

Av mannaz! (Have manners! Be polite!)
Se oudi-duu! (Say howdy! How d'you do?)

Gud maanin. Good morning. (Some just say, *"Maanin."*)
Gud eevnin. Good evening. (Reg.: *Gud iivlin,* pronounced *"good eevlin."*)
Gud aafta nuun. Good afternoon. (Regional: *"Gud eevlin,"* instead.)

Ou yu du?	How are you? How do you do?
Gud, tanks. Ou yuu?	Fine, thanks. How about you?
Mi gud tu. A wa time now?	I'm good too. What time is it?
A wan a clak.	It's one o'clock.

Mi a goh shuoh goh watch "Star Wars" fwor-terty; yu nuoh weh di plaaza de? (I'm going to the movies to see "Star Wars"; do you know where the plazas are?)

Yu kiaa lass; di plaza wid di tieta de roun di kaana. (You can't lose your way; the plaza with the theater is around the corner.)

Tank yu, baas. Rispek! (Thanks, boss. Respect.)

PAAT TUU

(Part Two)

Prefix and Suffix Patterns

The Patwa Prefix

English	Patwa
under- (undercut)	*aanda- (aandakut)*
co- (coworker, cooperate)	*kwo-* or *kaa- (kwo werka, kaapariet)*
op- (opposition)	*ap-* or *op- (up puzzishan* or *appa zishan)* (Note: Patwa *op* sounds like English "up.")
un- (unusual) in- (input, same in Patwa) im- (immigrant, same in Patwa)	*an- (an-yuujwal)* Antonym prefixes are few in Patwa, because Patwa uses *"noh"* as a universal prefix to make opposites.
en- (ensure)	*en- (enshuor)*

The Patwa Suffix

English	Patwa
-ible (flexible, sensible)	*-ibl/ebl (flexebl/flexibl, sensebl)*
-ness (laziness, impoliteness)	*-niss (liezzinniss, fiestinniss)*
- hood (neighborhood)	*-wud (nieba wud)*
-ist, -ism (pianist, socialism)	*-iss, -izzim (pianis, swoshal izzim)*
-tion (precaution, reaction)	*-shan (prikaashan, riakshan)*

Since English has many more prefixes and suffixes than those in the tables above, it's good to know the Patwa equivalents have similar pronunciation:
ab-, anti-, bi-, circum-, de-, dis-, en-, ex-, -ful, -fy, in-, il-, im-, in-, mis-, non-. tri-, un-, uni-, -able, -ant, -ish, -ity, -ive, -ize, -ly, -ment, -ship, etc.

Other Endings

English -cal = -*kal*
logical = *lajjik-kal*
technical = *teknik-kal*

vowel + -sual = -*jual*
visual = *vijwal/vijual*

English -tuous = -*shos*
presumptuous = *prizzum-shos*

English -tual = -*tchual*
actual = *aktchual*
ritual = *rich (yu) wal*

English -ing = *in* or *n*
ceiling = *seelin*
wedding = *wedn*

English -tain = -*tn*
plantain = *plaantn*
curtain = *curtn*

English: -pathy = -*pati*
sympathy = *simpati*

English -tory* = -*tchrih*, -*teri*
factory = *fak-tchrih (fakchri)*
victory = *vik-tchrih (vikchri)*
mandatory = *manditeri*

English -ire = -*a-ya*:
retire = *ritta-ya*
require = *rikwa-ya*

vowel + -dual = -*jwal*
gradual = *grajwal*

English -tude = -*chuud*
aptitude = *aptichuud*

English -er/-or = -*a*
advisor = *advaï za*
spectator = *spektieta*

English -age = *ij*
manage = *mannij*
image = *imij*

English -ect/-act = -*ek/-ak*
circumspect = *sirkumspek*
impact = *impak*

English – ology = -*alaji*
theology = *tialaji*

English -tery = -*tchrih*
battery = *batch-ri*
lottery = *latchri*

*The *t* in front of standard *ch* reminds you Patwa *ch* is only as in "cheese."

Yu Neva Nuoh Yu Nuoh (You Didn't Know You Knew)

"Day" is *dieh* (standard spelling: *die*), but "today" and "yesterday" are *tudde (tude)* and *yessideh (yeside)*. Can you arrange these days from Sunday to Saturday?

Monde, Terzde, Sonde, Wenzde, Satde (or *Sattidde*), *Chuuzde, Fry-de (Frai de)*

1_____, 2_____, 3_____, 4_____, 5_____, 6_____, 7_____

Answer: 1.*Sondeh*, 2.*Mondeh*, 3.*Chuuzdeh*, 4.*Wenzdeh*, 5.*Terzdeh*, 6.*Fry-deh (Frai de)*, 7.*Satdeh (Satde/Satide*, or *Sattiddeh)*

FYI: "Every Sunday" is *evri Sonde*. While "on Sunday" can be translated to be *"pan Sonde,"* in Patwa, *"a Sonde-dieh* time" *(taim)* is "on Sunday**s**."

The Months *(Di Mont Dem)*

June and July sound the same in Patwa as in English. Here's more: *Jan-yuweri, Feb-yuweri, Maatch, Yepril, Mieh, Juun, July, Aagus, Septemba, Aktwoba, Novemba, Disemba* (In broken Patwa, *Septemba* is *"Sektemba."*)

Who, Where and What We Find on the Map

America is *America* (regional: *Merka*). These also sound the same in Patwa:

Africa/African, Bermuda/Bermudian, China/Chinese, Cuba/Cuban, Europe, French, Ghana, Germany/German, Greece/Greek, India/Indian, Italy/Italian, Japan/Japanese, Liberia/Liberian, Nigeria/Nigerian, Russia/Russian, Somalian, Sweden/Swedish, Swiss, Trinidad/Trinidadian, Zimbabwe

Can you guess these geographical names? *Aïalan, Baabiedoz/Biejan, Britn/British, Fraanss, Kianada/Kianiedian, Switsalan*

Answers: Ireland, Barbados/Barbadian, Britain/British, France, Canada/Canadian, Switzerland

Numerals: *Yu nuoh dem numba ya? Mek wi match dem!*
(Do you know these numbers? Let's match them!)

11	*terty*
1	*faaty*
30	*unjred (onjred)*
3	*touzn*
4	*tree (trii)*
100	*wan*
7	*fuor*
40	*sevn*
1,000	*ilevn*

Answer: 11/*ilevn*; 1/*wan*; 3/*tree*; 4/*fuor*; 100/*unjred*; 7/*sevn*; 40/*faaty*; 1,000/*touzn*; 30/*terty*

Yu Fievrit Kola (Your Favorite Colors)

"Kola" is pronounced like English "cull a" (not like the fizzy drinks). Primary is *praï-meri*. The primary colors are *red, bluu,* and *yelloh (yelo)*. "Secondary" is *sekanderi*. Secondary colors are *ariinj, griin,* and *perpl*. Red/blue/purple/brown/pink/green/black all sound the same as in English. *Si muor ya!* Here's more: *grieh, biej, wyt (waït), bergandi, maav, silva* and *guol*.(grey, beige, white, burgundy, mauve, silver and gold.)

Patwa Homophones

"Customer" and "stammer" rhyme in Patwa: *custamma/stamma (kostama/ stama)*. So do "Thomas" and "customers": *Tammass/custammass (Tamas/ kostamas)*. (**Reminder:** This book doubles Patwa consonants to show the shortness of vowels.) "Earth" and "concert" are *ert and kansert*. "Void" and "side" rhyme with "wide"; "coarse/course and worst": *kwoss, woss*. "Hurdle, girdle and curdle" rhyme with gurgle: *grrgl*. Here's more:

at, hat, hurt and hot = *at*	bare, beer and bear = *bier*
bottle and battle = *bakl*	bondage and bandage = *bandij*
close (shut) and clothes = *cluōz*	fear, fare and fair = *fier*
goal and gold = *guol*	half and off = *aaf*
grater and greater = *grieta*	handle and angle = *angl*
old, whole, hold and hole = *wol*	order and harder = *aada*
quote, court and coat = *kwut*	share, shear and sheer = *shier*
through, true and chew = *choo*	wear and ware = *wier*
whirl and world = *werl*	wield and wheel = *weel*
wrist and risk = *riss*	yarn and yawn = *yaan*

Pliers and a prayer rhyme with tires *(pla-yaz, pra-yaz, ta-yaz)*. "Hire" and "fire" have that same hard "i" sound: "hire" = *I-ya;* "fire" = *fa-ya (faïa)*.

One ear is *wan yez (iez)*.
Two ears are *tuu yez*.

One flower is *wan flouaz*.
Two flowers are *tuu flouaz*.

One tooth is *wan teet*.
Two teeth are *tuu teet*.

One hand is *wan an*.
Two hands are *tuu an*.

A foot is a *fut*, but a shoe is a *shuuz*, and shoelaces are *shuuzliess*. Jan Poblik's two shoes are *tuu shooz*, but his two feet are *tuu fut*. *Jan Poblik* (John Public) in Patwa means "the general public."

Mi a di fos Jomiekan we liv a Timbuktu. Gud! Im av tuu kozn we liv de tu.

"I'm the first Jamaican who lives in Timbuktu. Good! He has two cousins who live there too."

Frequent Elision: How the Words "Run Together"

Consider, "It's a good company to work for." Patwa: *A wan gud kompini fi wok fa.* The elision links *wan* and *gud*. A native speaker says, *"A waŋgud kompini fi wok fa."* Like the English contractions (e.g., it's, he's), quite often the elision or "liaison" is a contraction: *goh alang* is *gallang*; *goh aan* (go on) is *gwaan*; *mi didda* (I was…) is *miida*; *mi did* is *miid*; *dem didda* is *demidda*. See Figure 1.1:

The Liaison — Figure 1.1

- *for it:* fih + it = feet — *Dem aaks feet.* (They asked for it.)
- *see it:* sih + it = seet — *Seet deh!* See it there! (There it is!)
- *go to:* goh + a = gaa — *Mi gaa church.* (I go to church.)
- *give it:* gih + it = geet — *Geet to ar*/Give it to her.
- *You are / You're:* yu + a = yaa — *Weh yaa du?* (What're you doing?)
- *Do it:* du + it = dweet — *Dweet!* (Do it!)
- *You're going:* yu + a goh = yaagoh
- *Doesn't have: Dem naav/it.* They don't have it. — noh + a/av = naa/naav

Note: "What you are doing?" = *Weh yaadu?* Standard: *feet/geet/seet/dweet = fiit/giit/siit dwiit*

Figure 1.2

The Liaison
Here's more of the Patios Liaison, to simplify it for you.

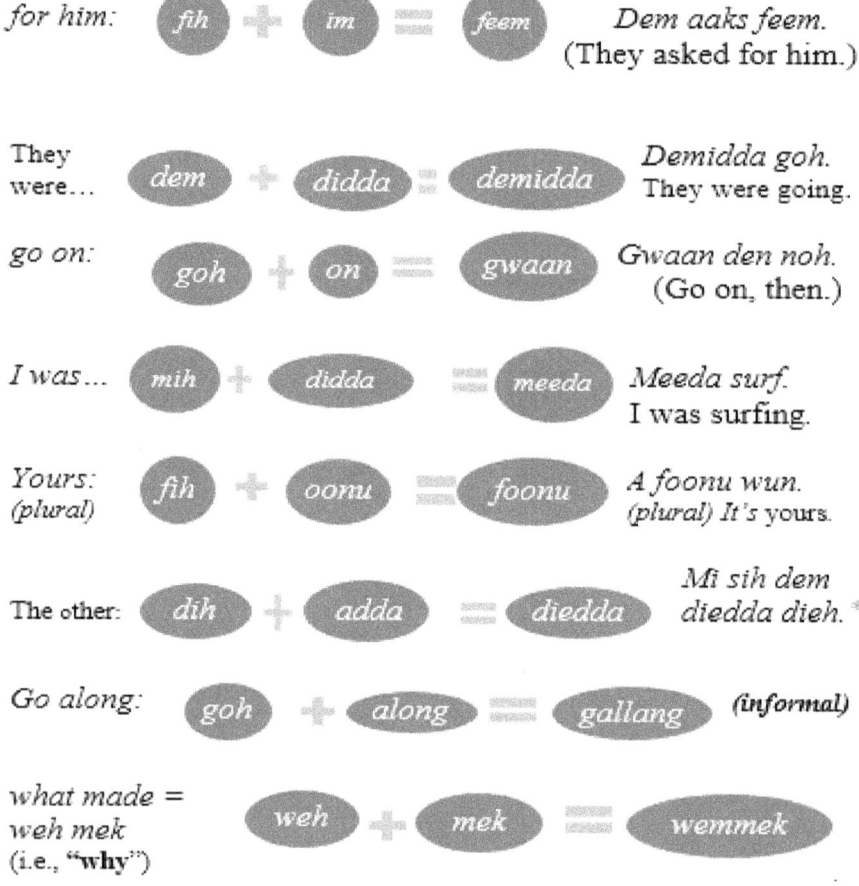

*"I saw them the other day." (Also: *Mi si dem dieda die.*)
Standard: *feem/meeda/foonu/wemmek = fiim/miida/fuunu/wemek*

Test Your Skill! *(Tes yu skill!)*

Draw a line to match the English word to its Patwa translation.

1. orange   yelloh (yelo)

2. purple   red

3. red   green (griin)

4. green   perpl

5. yellow   arreenj (ariinj)

Answers: 1. arreenj; 2. perpl; 3. red; 4. green; 5. yelloh

What are these words in English?

Mek wi ges! (Let's guess!)

1. kiat/daag   2. kiebl/dwor   3. kiabbij/glaa-siz

4. bliem/towzn   5. kiap/anbag   6. tiebl/kantin-yu

7. naav/naa   8. dweet/seet   9. yaago/geet

Answers: 1. cat/dog; 2. cable/door; 3. cabbage/glasses; 4. blame/thousand; 5. cap/handbag; 6. table/continue; 7. doesn't have/not; 8. do it/see it; 9. you're going/give it

Pieces of Immersion

Fun & Games in Patwa: A modified version of dodgeball is called *dandy-shandy* in Patwa. A game of "tag" is *stucky* (sometimes played as *"laas lik"*). Soccer is *futbaal*.

Riddles: *Rigl mi dis, an rigl mi dat. Ges mi dis rigl, an parraps nat.* (Riddle me this, and riddle me that. Guess me this riddle, and perhaps not.)

Mi spred mi bed, an briiz blwoh it mek it pull-up. Mi bed a wa?
I spread my bed, and the breeze blew it and made a mess of it. What's my bed?

Tan up bakka mi; tan up in fronta mi; yu neva-yet inna mi wieh.
Stand behind me; stand before me; you're never in my way.

Ou plantn difrent fram tiela?
How is a plantain different from a tailor?

Answers: *kloud (*the clouds*), shado* (shadow), *Plantn fit fi cut, tiela cut fi fit.* A plantain is fit to cut; tailors cuts to fit.

A Comical Conversation

Jim: *Mi fren, yu jos se yaav sopm impuotant fi tell mi. A wa?*
    (My friend, you just said you've got something important to tell me. What is it?)

Bim: *Mi noh memba – oh, mi memba.* (I don't remember – oh, I remember.)
Jim: *Tell mi den. Weh yaa taak bout?* (Then tell me. What are you talking about?)
Bim: *Shuor – oops! Mi figget agen.* (Sure – oops! I forgot again!)

A Word to Remember: *Weh* (What, Where, or Away)

Weh yaa taak bout? Weh yu niem?
(What're you talking about? What's your name?)
Weh yaa du?   We yu goh?   (What're you doing? Where did you go?)
Weh yu se?   Weh yaa se?   (What did you say? What're you saying?)
Weh yu liv?   Mi liv a Paris. (Where do you live? I live in Paris.)
Weh im de?   Im get weh.   (Where is he? He got away.)
Weh yu meen? Ou yu meen? (What do you mean? How do you mean?)

Parts of Speech

Articles

Indefinite English articles (**both** "a" **and** "an") can be *a* or ***wan**,* in Patwa:

Mi waa wan shuuz: I want **a** pair of shoes.

Gwaan bunx a chuun noh. Start/continue playing **a** song/tune.
("*Gwaan du...*" can mean "begin doing [in the interim] ..." or "keep doing...")

Popular Patlish expression: *It was wan peess a sopm!* "It was a spectacle!" ("It was a piece of something.") Patwa: *Mi se; a wan peess a sopm!* "I'm telling you; it was a spectacle!"

The English definite article "the" is *di* (pronounced like the "di-" in "dip").
Example: *Paass di nex tambrin.* Pass me the other/next tamarind.
Note: "The other" is also *di adda*, contracted to become *diedda* (the liaison).

Demonstratives

this = *dis*   **that** = dat

this one = *da wan ya* (regionally, *deh wan ya*)

that one = *da wan de* (regionally, *de wan de*)

these = *dem... ya* (You might hear *deez* in Patlish.)

Example: *dem book ya:* these books*; dem bag ya:* these bags

these ones = *dem wan ya*

those = *dem... de* (You might hear *dwuz* in Patlish.)

those ones = *dem wan de*

Example: *dem stwuv de:* those stoves*; dem frak de:* those dresses

You may hear Patlish nudging the verb and article like this, in everyday speech:

Patlish: *Dem is a uopless kiess.*

Patwa: ***Dem a*** *wan uopless kies.* (They are a hopeless case.)

The likely Patwa response is either of these:

Dem noh uopless. They are not hopeless.

Dem uopless fi chuu. They're truly hopeless.

Dem noh uopless nonataal. They're not at all hopeless.

The Demonstrative Ending

Demonstratives find themselves at the end of most Patwa statements. You'll hear this old British construct in every Jamaican community:

A juok dat. = A joke, that.

(*A juok yaa mek.* = You're joking.)

A difrant/difrent ting dat. = A different thing, that.

A rigl dat. = A riddle, that one.

(*Da wan de a rigl.* = That one is a riddle.)

A gud book dis. = A good book, this. (Paraphrase: This is a good book.)

The wording of those examples is simple. This kind of "Star Wars" Yoda transposition is standard and popular in Patwa. Consider these:

A faass dem faass. Nosy is what they are.
A muss a ramp yaa ramp. You must be playing.
A mussi ramp yaa ramp. (Literally: It must be playing you're playing.)

A fi ar kiamra dat? Is that her camera? (Literally: Is it her camera, that?")

Personal Pronouns

Subject Pronouns

I = *mi*	*Mi si.* I see. (Patlish: *A si.*)
you = *yu*	*Yu goh.* You go.
she = *shi*	*Shi nuoh.* She knows
he = *im*	*Im aaks im.* He asked him.
it = *it*	*It noh dun.* It is not done.
we = *wi*	*Wi choss dem som pants lent.* (We credited them some trouser-fabric.)
you (pl.) = *oonu/unu*	*Im kiaan tell unu notn/nutn.* He can't tell you *[pl]* anything.
they = *dem*	*Dem a sampl.* They're indescribable.

Object Pronouns

me = *mi*	us = *wi*
you = *yu*	you (pl.) = *oonu/unu*
her = *ar* (Only *ar* differs from the subject.) him = *im* it = *it*	them = *dem* (regardless of gender)

Examples

Mi dweet fi dem. Dem dweet fi mi. (I did it for them. They did it for me.)

Dem tell wi se dem aggo trien wi, an wi wi trien unu -- soh dem se. (They told us they're going to train us, and we will train you (pl) -- so they say.) Note: "*Se*" in this context is "that" and then "say"; also, "*wi wi*" is "we will."

The English "she" is used as an emphatic object pronoun. *"A wa du ar?"* shows concern for the well-being of a girl/woman, but when the asker is annoyed, you'll hear, *"A wa du shee?"* (What's up with her?) *Wa rang wid shee?* (What's wrong with her?) Also *yu, mi,* and *wi* (*"Wa rang wid **yuu**?"*).

Pronoun Adjectives

my = *mi, fi mi*	our = *wi, fi wi*
your = *yu, fi yu* (Patlish: *yer*)	your (plural) = *oonu/unu, fuunu*
his = *im; feem; fi im*	their = *dem, fi dem* (regardless of
hers = *ar, fi ar*	its = *fiit* (feet: *fi + it"*) *fi it uon*/own

Example: *Watch yu step. A fi yu bizniz.* (Watch your step. It's your business.)
Example: *Dem fix dem TV.* (They fixed their TV.)
Example: *A fuunu ous dat?* (Is that *(pl.)* your house?)

Possessive Pronouns

mine = *fi mi*	ours = *fi wi*
yours = *fi yu* (*yern/yers*)	yours (*pl.*) = *fuunu (fi + unu/*
his = *fi im (feem)*, hers = *fi*	theirs = *fi dem*

Example: *A fi yu?* Is it yours? (*A fi mi.* It's mine.)
Example: *A fi ar uon.* It's hers (her own).
Note: Patwa has no apostrophe S: *A Kim aada.* It's Kim's order.

Reflexive Pronouns

(All persons are *"self"* -- even in plural.)

myself = *misself*	ourselves = *wisself*
yourself = *yu self*	yourselves = *unu self (pl.)*
herself = *ar self*	She herself said. *Sh<u>ee</u> ar self*
himself = *imself* itself = *itself*	He himself said… *Im imself se…*
themselves = *demself*	They themselves said… *Dem*

Prepositions

English says, "look at." Patwa says, *look pan* (look upon).

on = *pan* (from "upon") *"pan tapa (tings)"* = "on top of (things)"
at = *de, a* (e.g., *Mi de a mi yaad*/I'm at home)
of = *a* (e.g., *Piis a kiek de pan di pliet.* A piece of cake is on the plate.)
beside = *sy-da* ("side of")   **behind** = *bakka*
for = *fi* (or *"fa"* ending a statement)   **before** *(prep.)* = *(een-) fronta*
in = *een, inna*   **out** = *out, outta*
from = *fram* (e.g., *Weh yu get it fram?* "Where did you get it [from]?")
to = *tu* (e.g., Give it to her. *Gi'it [geet] to ar.* [more commonly: *Gih ar.*])

Examples

*Goh fram ya soh **tu** de soh.* (Go from here to there.)
*Mi a goh **a** wan seminar.* (I'm going **to** a seminar *[gaa seminar]*.)

Mi a leff it inna dat; a it mi did a luk fa. (I'm leaving it in that; it's what I was looking for.)

Oo yaa luk fa in de? Yu naa goh wova de soh? (Whom are you looking for, in there? Aren't you going over there?)

Yeh, yu noh si se a dat mi a du? (Yes, don't you see that's what I'm doing?)

Yu si wan man paas ya soh? (Did you see a man pass by here?)

Mi si plenty peepl. Ou im luk? Im taal aar im shaat? Maaga aar fat? (I saw many people. How does he look? Is he tall or is he short? Skinny or fat?)

Im midiom – avrij. (He's of medium build – average.)

Oo im fieva? (Whom does he favor [i.e., resemble; look like]?)

Im fieva imself. (He looks like himself.)

(Adverbs related to this topic: here = *ya* or *ya-soh*; there = *de* or *de-soh*.)

Omission of Preposition

"I go to my house" is *Mi goh a mi yaad (gaa mi yaad)*. There is no preposition in "I go home," since "home" means "to my residence." This parallels Patwa (e.g., *Mi goh wom.* = I go home.)
Im goh dakta. (He goes/went to the doctor.)

Dem goh school. (They go/went to school.)

Mi goh maakit. (I go/went to the market. Also: *Mi gaa maakit.*)

Note this Interrogative Pronoun: **Whose** *(oofa/uufa; fi oofa/uufa)*

A oofa? A oofa uon? (Literally: "It's whose own?")

A fi oofa? (Literally: "It's for whom?"). *A fi oo?* (Whom is it meant for?)

Conjunctions

Some coordinators and other conjunctions are the same as in English. Except for phrases such as *siekka dat* or *choo dat*, the list is close to English.

an = and

aar = or

by (bai) = by

yet-still = yet

aafta = after

eevn doh = even though

kaa = because

den = then

chuu dat = because of that

se = that

but (bot) = but

bifuor = before

if = if

soh = so

dwoh = though; *alduo*/although

a dat mek = as a result of that

bikkaa = because

soh langss = as long as

siekka dat = because of that

in kies = in case; in the event that

Examples
Dem tell mi se a fwor it staat. (They told me that it starts/started at four.)
Dem lef, chuu im liet. (They left, because he was late.)
A kaa dem kudn wiet. (It's because they couldn't wait.)

Note: In Patwa, "*but*" is the same as "however, nonetheless," etc.
Dwoh is the same as "in spite of, despite, etc. (also spelt *duo*: **one** syllable).
Kaa is the conjunction "for": *Mi naa fret, kaa mi win.* (I'm not fretting, for I won.)
English "since" means and sounds the same in Patwa (spelt differently).

PAAT TRII

(Part Three)

Verbs

Verb stems are often entire verbs. Below, *fi* is "to": *Mi tell you fi goh.* ("I told you to go."). Here, lower-case *u* for *unu* reminds you the "u" is short.

To Be: *Fi Bi* (Pronounce the verb *a* and the pronoun as one word, e.g., *wia*.)

I am… = *Mi a… (pronounced mia)*	We are… = *Wi a…*
You are… = *Yu a…*	You *(pl)* are …. = ***unu** a…*
She/him/it is… = *Shi/im/it a…*	They are… = *Dem a…*

There's no Patwa equivalent of this sentence: "I am," but **Patlish** says, "*Mi is.*"

To Be: *Fi De* (When "referring to location, the infinitive "to be" is *fi de*.)

I am here = *Mi de ya.*	We are here. = *Wi de ya.*
You are here. = *Yu de ya.*	You *(pl)* are here. = ***unu** de ya.*
She/him/it is here. = *Shi/im/it de ya.*	They are here. = *Dem de ya.*

To Make: *Fi Mek*

I make. = *Mi mek.*	We make. = *Wi mek.*
You make. = *Yu mek.*	You make. = ***unu** mek* (Plural)
She/he/it makes. = *Shi/im/it mek.*	They make. = *Dem mek.*

To Want: *Fi Waa* (This also means "**to want to**.")

I want. = *Mi waa.*	We want. = *Wi waa.*
You want. = *Yu waa.*	You (pl) want. = ***unu** waa.*
She/he/it wants. = *Shi/im/it waa.*	They want. = *Dem waa.*

To Do: *Fi Du*

I do… = *Mi du*…	We do… = *Wi du*…
You do… = *Yu du*…	You do. = ***unu** du*… (Plural)
She/he/it does… = *Shi/im/it*	They do… = *Dem du*…

When it's a two-word statement, use Patlish *duu*: "They do." = *Dem duu*.

To Go: *Fi Goh* (can also mean to go **to** [do something])

I go. = *Mi goh*.	We go. = *Wi goh*.
You go. = *Yu goh*.	You go. = ***unu** goh*. (Plural)
She/him/it goes. = *Shi/im/it goh*.	They go. = *Dem goh*.

FYI: "It's like that." = *It goh soh*. "That's how it goes." = *A soh it goh*.

To Have: *Fi Av*

I have. = *Mi av*.	We have. = *Wi av*.
You have. = *Yu av*.	You have. = ***unu** av*. (Plural)
She/he/it has. = *Shi/im/it av*.	They have. = *Dem av*.

To Stand: *Fi Stanop*	**To Sit**: *Fi Sidong*	**To Enjoy:** *Fi Enjaai*
To Live: *Fi Liv*	**To Die:** *Fi Ded*	**To Exhaust:** *Fi Exaastid*
To Say: *Fi Se*	**To Call:** *Fi Kaal*	**To Break:** *Fi Brok*
To Speak: *Fi Taak*	**To Take:** *Fi Tek*	**To Remember:** *Fi Memba*
	To Leave: *Fi Lef*	**To Give:** *Fi Gi*

Example of *Fi Waa* and *"It a…"*:

Mi waa liv; mi waa drink saril; it a (gwaan) draw. (I want **to** live; I want **to** drink sorrel; it's drawing/steeping.)

Adverbs

As in English, some words are adverbs *and* adjectives (e.g., walking *fast*; a *fast* car; *a waak faass; wan faass kiar*) in Patwa. Our intensifiers and descriptive patterns are lively. You hear Patwa's ancestral Akan Twi, when repetition often replaces some English "-ly" endings. For example, "fast" is *faass*, but "very fast" is *faass-faass*; "slowly" is *slwo-slwo*. Also, this seems counterintuitive: When something is very nice, we say it "nice bad" *(naïs bad)*. Here's more:

They ate it immediately. *Dem niam it kwik-kwik.* ("Quickly" in Patlish is *kwik-time,* but there's **no** "*slwoh-time,*" intuitive though it might seem).
We were walking slowly: *Wi did a-waak slwo-slwo.*
She pulled it together nicely: *Shi katch it up nice-nice (naïs naïs).*
That usually happens; they do it gladly: *Dat yuujali apn; dem dweet gladly.*

Adjectives

Positive	Comparative	Superlative
intrestin (interesting)	*muor intrestin/intrestin bad*	*muos intrestin*
plien (plain)	*pliena/plien-plien*	*plieniss*
nuff/nof (plentiful)	*nuffa/nuff-nuff (nof nof)*	*nuffiss (nofes)*
sieff (safe)	*sieffa/sief-sief*	*sieffiss* (safest)
faar (far)	*ferda/faara* (further/farther)	*faa-ress/faar-faar*

Fi Exaampl (For Example)
Dat tek nuff-nuff time (nof nof taïm). That takes a huge amount of time.
Dis a di muos dillishos axtiell. This is the most delicious oxtail.
Notn noh sweeta dan shuga kien. Nothing's sweeter than sugarcane.
Dem reech faara (furda) dan di ress. They reached farther than the rest.

Present Tense

Subject plus verb stem equals present tense: "*Unu nuoh -- unu nuoh?*" (*pl.* "You know -- do you know?") Subject/adjective sentences need no copula in Patwa. "Is" is implied: "*Dat gud.*" (That is good.) *Dat noh gud.* (That's not good.) *Dem invalv inna it. Aaks im if im invalv.* ("They're involved in it. Ask him if he is involved.") Subject/noun statements need *a*: *Dem a sient.* ("They are saints.") *Dat a di ting.* "That's the thing." For example:

Mi de ya chuu mi lov Patwa. I'm here, because I love Patwa.

Dem noh goh shuo noh muor. They don't go to the movies any more.

Mi goh nof time. Mi noh nuo weh niem taiad. I go many times. I'm never tired. (The idiom literally means: "I don't know what's named 'tired'").

Sum peepl noh andastan di werl. Some people don't understand the world. *Som siev; som noh nuoh ou fi siev.* Some save; some don't know how to save.

Weneva wok staat, dem run weh. Whenever work starts, they run away.

Dem daanss gud dwoh. They dance well, though.

Yeh, man, wi kian daanss tu. Yes, we can dance too.

Im jos lieh dung de. He just lies there. He just lay there.

Di present tenss simpl soh till. The present tense is extremely simple. *Dem sentenss ya a sopn elss.* These sentences are something else

FYI: Patwa has a popular pattern of **"*kum*" + main verb.**

Im kum push up imself pan dem. He pushed himself on them.

Patlish *"Das"* **FYI:** *Das gud. Das nat gud.* That's good. That isn't good.

Patwa: *Dat noh gud.* "That's not good."

Future Tense

The future tense in English adds "will" or "to be going to (do)." Patwa is similar. "Going to (do)" is *"aggo" (aggo)* or *"gwaïn"*; "will" is *"wi."* *"Aggo,"* meaning "is/am/are going to (do)" equates to American "gonna."

Yu nuotis? Did you notice? "Will" in Patwa is *wi* (like the first-person plural pronoun).

Mi wi dweet. Dem wi goh.	I will do it. They will go.
Wi wi get a gud ansa.	We shall get a favorable answer.
Mi nuo yu aggo av fun wid Patwa.	I know you're going to have fun with Patwa.
Yaago luv it. (yu + aggo)	You're going to love it.
Mi aggo falla di ruul.	I'm going to follow the rules.
Mi aggo look **or** *"gwyin look."*	I'm going to look.
Dem aggo goh, nex week.	They're going to go, next week.
Im aggo tek it, Terz-deh.	He's going to take it, on Thursday.
Im naago tek it, Terzde.	He isn't going to take it, Thursday.

A Conversation for Example

Wemmek dem dress up soh?	Why are they dressed up like that?
Dem a goh out.	They're going out (on the town).
Dem out fi leff.	They're about to leave.
Mi aggo aaks dem wai.	I'm going to ask them why.
Noh aaks dem.	Don't ask them.
Aaraït. Mi naago aaks.	Alright, I'm not going to ask.

Note: To avoid confusion with English, we aren't using the standard spelling for *"aggo'* (a-g-o). The "o" in Patwa "aggo" has a very short "o" sound as in *"son."*

Past Tense

Past tense and present tense are much the same in Patwa, but for the optional *"did"* that can precede the verb in the past tense. In English and Patwa, "did" can emphasize a past action; however, the Patwa *"did"* mostly makes it clear that we are referring to the past. Here's the past tense:

Mi goh.	I went.
Mi a goh, tu-de.	I am going, today. (Regional: *tiddeh*.)
Mi goh, yessideh (yeside).	I went, yesterday.

Remember the elision ("Patwa Liaison") is in everything:

Mi + did becomes *mi + id*, which becomes *meed (miid)*.

Mi aggo goh.	I'm going to go.
Mi did aggo goh.	I was going to go.
Meed aggo goh.	I was going to go.
Mi did goh yessideh.	I went, yesterday.

Mi 'id goh, yessideh. = *Meed goh, yessideh.* = I went yesterday.

Meed aggo goh yessideh, boh mi chienj mi plan. Mi neva badda goh. I was going to go, yesterday, but I changed my plans. I didn't bother to go.

Regionally: The "t" might get dropped from "but" as in, *"Dem kaal, boh meeda sleep."* ("They called, but I was sleeping.")

More:
Wi didda goh. = *Wi 'idda goh.* = *Weeda goh.* = We were going.
Weeda goh Jumieka. We were going to Jamaica.
Shi didda plan fi fly out tumaro. = *Sheeda plan fi fly out tumaro.*

"She was planning on flying 'catching a flight' tomorrow."

The Continuous Tense
A Reflection of Older English

Quaint words[6] such as *"bitwix"* for "between" and *"maaly* gripe" for "illness" remain in <u>rural</u> Patwa. However, we hear "antique" English (*maids a-milking, lords a-leaping, etc.)* in the continuous tense, in **all** of Patwa. We simply drop the "-ing" ending and keep the prefix *"a"* – dropping the "ing" is important.

Wi a goh.	We're a-going. (Modern English: We're going.)
Dem a daanss.	They're a-dancing. (They're dancing.)
Dem a kum.	They're a-coming. (They're coming)
Wi a waak.	We're a-walking. (We're walking.)
Wi si wan ship a siel.	We saw a ship a-sailing. (We saw a ship sailing.)

Popular phrases in the continuous:

A dat mi a se.	That's what I'm saying.
A dat mi a du.	That's what I'm doing.
A yuu mi a taak.	I'm talking to (or referring to) you.

Rurally, *"a"* is *da* or *de*: *"Mi da goh."* (I'm going.) Unlike Patlish, **the Patwa continuous has no "ing."** *Intrestin, tryin, willin, sneekin, fiteeggin* and *taakin* are adjectives/nouns: *"Dat tuu dazlin; mi naa wier it."* (That's too dazzling; I'm not wearing it.) *"Yu gi tu much taakin!"* (You elicit too much reproach — too much scolding/talking.)

---

[6] You can learn more about Patwa's various influences in Frederic Gomes Cassidy's *Jamaica Talk: Three Hundred Years of the English language in Jamaica* University Press of the West Indies, 1961.

Nuances from Tense to Tense

Take a good look at the contrasts below, as nuances become clearer:

Mama goh church. (Mama gaa church.) Mom goes to or attends church.

Weh shi goh? Where did she go? Where does she go?

A weh yu anti did goh? Where did your aunt go?

A church shi goh. It was to church she went. Also: It is to church she goes.

Im kozn a goh a church (*a gaa church*). His cousin is going to church.

Wan time shi did a goh church (*yuus tu goh*). Once, she used to go to church.

A wan time im daata goh. His daughter went one time only.

Shi did a goh (*shiida goh*) *church, dem time de.* She attended church, back then ("in those times"). Regionally, "church" is also "*chutch*"; also, regionally, *wenna* or *enna* replaces *didda*.

In Patlish, you'll hear "*wozza*" which means "was -*ing*." *Wozza waak* means "was walking." *Is where shi wozza goh?* "Where was she going?"

Vokabuleri (Vocabulary)

There were many references to family/*fambili,* on this page. Here's a guide:

madda; faada (vulg.: muma; pupa) = mother; father

daata; son = daughter; son

son-in-laa; daata-in-laa = son-in-law; daughter-in-law

step-son; step-daata = step-son, step-daughter

niis (neess); neviu; anti; onkl; kozn = niece; nephew; aunt; uncle; cousin

gran-son; grandaata = grandson; granddaughter

granmadda/grani; granfaada/grampa = grandmother/granny; grandfather/grandpa

Patwa and the English Participial Phrase

Apart from the adage, *"Libbatti-tekkin kum choo kiellissniss"* (the taking of liberties comes through carelessness), there aren't many complete equivalents of gerund and participial English phrases in Patwa. There are paraphrases such as the infinitive structure. For example:
Having good health is crucial.
Gud elt kruu-shal (fi av). (Good health is crucial [to have].)
It kruu-shal fi av gud elt. (It's crucial to have good health.)

Consider these:
The man selling mangoes cherishes the mango walk (orchard).
Di man weh a sell mango cherish di mango waak. (Literally: The man *what*)
Di mango venda cherish di mangoh waak. (The mango vendor cherishes…)
Start dancing. *Staat daanss.*
I am/was already doing it: *Mi did/dun a dweet (a reddy).*
I am/was already going. *Mi dun a goh.*
When I was ironing, there was an outage. *Wen miida aian, light lak aaf.*

Filler Words

On to another topic: Where did Patwa filler words come from?
a = (starting filler)   *Ee?* = Eh? Huh?   *noh* = (persuading)
issi = y'see   *e-yer* = y'hear (*yaa*)   *innoh* = y'know   *aam* = um

Consider *"ee?"* our mild exclamation with a question mark (?) that's often rhetorical. Everything being remarked on gets an *"ee?"* at the end: *It priti ee?* "Isn't it pretty?" *It priti, noh chuu?* "It's pretty, isn't it?"

You'll also hear it in mild sarcasm or humor: *Dem gud ee? Dem a sopm elss. Dem tek aal a it an noh leff non fi noh badi elss.* ("They're horrid. They're something else. They took it all and left none for anyone else.")

Understand the many meanings of "a":

Do you know the classic General Echo song "Arlene"? If you do, then you know this Patwa line that begins with filler *a*: *A wan jenaral inna di yaad.* "There's one general in the yard: only one ruler."

Here are other statements that begin with *a*.

A fi ar.	It's hers.
A it dat.	That's it.
A it dat?	Is that it?
Mi a ga wan miitn.	I'm going to a meeting.
A noh nottn.	It's nothing; no big thing. No offense taken.

Understanding "*dunt*":

Dunt? = Isn't it? Aren't they? Don't you think so? (*Dunt it? Dwun?*)

Da shuoh de intrestin, dunt (duont it)? That show's interesting, isn't it?

Dunt is from the word "don't" but is equivalent to informal British "*innit.*"

Yaa: This is used to coax, but can either reinforce or soften an imperative.

Kum, yaa. = Come. (**Not**: *Kum ya.* "Come here.") *Gwaan, yaa!* = Go.

FYI: A Neat Phrase to Know

Nat tu dat. Not largely. *Yu riet dem? Nat tu dat.* Do your rate them? Not much. *A dat mi se tu.* I agree. (That's what I'm saying too.)

Antonym Prefix

Opposites in Patwa use *"noh"* or in a few instances the *"an-"* prefix:

"Uncalled for" is *an-kaalfa* or *noh kaalfa*, as in, *"Dat noh kaalfa."* Idiomatically: *Wa fi yu kiaa bi an-fi yu.* (What's yours can't be un-yours.)

"Usual" is *yuujal* or *yuujwal*, and "unusual" is *an-yuujwal*.

"Grateful" is *griet-ful*, and "ungrateful" is *an-grietful*.

Other common examples of antonym prefix words in Patwa are:
an-waantid, an-nesiseri, an-billiivebl (unwanted, unnecessary, unbelievable)
incansidarret (inconsiderate)
disrispekful (disrespectful)

Moods: Ability and Obligation

In English, two tone-structures express ability: "can + the verb stem (e.g., I can win)" and "to be able + infinitive (e.g., I am able to win)." In Patwa, there are also two ways to express ability: "*kian* + the verb stem" or "*yebl* + infinitive."

Mi kian win, or: *"Mi yebl fi win."* (I can win/I'm able to win.)

Mi kian goh, (I can go) or: *"Mi yebl fi goh."* (I'm able to go.)

To negate, replace *kian* with *kiaan(t)* or put *noh* before *yebl*:
Mi kiaa goh. I can't go. *Mi kiangoh.* I can go.

Mi noh yebl fi goh. I'm unable to go.

To express that you're obliged to do something:
Use the stem of the verb "*fi av*" plus the stem of the relevant verb.
To have to = *fi av fi* (with liaison: *av + fi = afi*)

Example: *Mi afi goh.* "I have to go."

You can also use *muss (mos)*:

Example: *Mi muss win.* "I must win."

Re the infinitive: In English, we say "to love to do" something. In Patwa, there's no "to" in that expression. *Im lov goh skuul.* "He loves to go to school."

The Subjunctive

A quick way to grasp pronunciation in the subjunctive in Patwa is to think of it as an informal loanword – coulda/*kudda* (*kuda*) for "could have"; *shuda* for "should have"; *wudda* (*wuda*) for "would have"; and *myta* (*mai-ta*) for "might have." For "should," Patwa uses *fi* more often than *shuda*. *Yu fi wiet!* "You ought to wait!" Prepositions and other words can sound informal too: *outta* for "out"; *inna* for "in"; gimme (*gimi*) for "give me"; and *leggo* (*lego*) for "let go".

Mi shuda goh.	I should go (or have gone).
Mi shuda did goh.	I should have gone.
ooda/uda	Would've been… *Dat uda gud.* That would/would've been good.
Yu fi spwut dem.	You should take them places.

Yu fi sopuot yu teem (supuot yu tiim). You should support your team.
Dem fi siev fi dem wol yej (uol iej). They should save for their old age.

The Interrogative

The interrogative is where lovers of Patwa's cadence play with intonation. Inflection changes declarative to interrogative, in statement questions.

A fi ar. It's hers.   *A fi ar?* Is it hers*?*

A fi ar wun/uon. It's her own.   *A fi ar wun?* Is it her own?

A feem van. It's his van.   *A feem van?* Is it his van?

A yuu. (*A yu!*) It's you.   *A yuu?* Is it you?

The "*a*" in those questions are necessary, unlike these you'll often hear:

A oo dat? Who is that? (Likewise: *Oo [uu] dat?* Who is that?)

A oofa van? Whose van is it? (Whose is "*oofa*" in Patwa *[uu-fa]*.)

A oofa uon? Whose is it? (*Uon* (own) rhymes with "fun" -- the English word.) *A yer sopm dem de?* Are those yours? (A *yern*. It's yours. *A fi yu.*) This is one point where Patwa hugs Patlish. We all use *yers* and *yern* often.

Oo yu awiet **fa***? Y'awiet* **fi** *dem?* For whom are you waiting? For them? To be "waiting for" is like the English "await." **Awiet**: *Mi awiet.* "I'm waiting."

When you ask the person who answered the door, "Who is it?" can be "*A oo?*" (Patlish: *"Is oo?"*) Answering the door yourself, "Who is it?" is *"Oo dat?"*

Yu nuo bout it. Weh yu nuo bout it? (You know about it; what do you know about it?)
"How do you…" is "*Ou yu*": How do you do that? = *Ou yu du dat?*

Verb/Noun Inversion for the Interrogative

A it dat? Is that all there is?
A it dat. That's it. That's all there is.
Note a nuance between *"a it dat"* and *"a dat"* described below:

A dat. That's what it is.   *A dat?* Is that what it is?

Dat a Kim. That's Kim.   *A Kim dat?* Is that Kim?

The Ws of Journalism

why = *wemmek* or *ow-kom* or *wai*	what = *weh* or *wa*
where = *weh* or "*wish paat*"	which = *wish; wich*
when = *wen*	how = **ou** (*ow*)

Declarative: *Dem kiatch/ketch a flight (flaït)*. They caught a flight.
A wen dem ketch a flight? When did they catch a flight? (Filler: "A")
Den ou dem ketch a flight? How did they catch a flight? (Filler: "then")
Weh dem ketch di flight (fram)? Where did they catch the flight (from)?
Wai/wemmek dem ketch a flight? Why did they/what made them catch a flight?
"Why?" by itself is "*Wai?*" Otherwise, we often say, "*Wemmek?*"

Wai yu noh se notn? (*Wemmek yu noh se notn?*) Why didn't you say anything? What for? = *Fi wa?* "Why won't you?" = *Wammek?* or *Wa stap yu?*

What's there to stop you? *Wa fi stap yu?* (With filler: *Den a wa fi stap yu?*)
"Why don't you?" is "Why don't you do it?" *Wai yu noh dweet?*

The Imperative (All the imperative requires is the verb stem.)

Stan up! Stand!	*Siddung!* Sit!
(Bih) kwa-yat! (Be) quiet!	*Stap giez!* Stop gazing!
Liddung! Lieh dung! Lie down!	*Gwaan!* **or** *Goh!* Go!
Wiet! Memba dis! Wait! Remember this!	*(Noh) dweet!* (Don't) do it!
Regional: *Stap giez!* =*Tap giez!* *Stap di naiz!* = *Tapi naiz!* = Stop the noise!	

The Negative

> *"Noh"* or *"duoh"* in front of any word negates it.
>
> *(Noh) goh!* = (Don't) go!   *(Noh) dweet!* = (Don't) do it!
>
> Patlish: *Duoh goh!* = Don't go!   Patlish: *Duoh dweet.* = Don't do it.
>
> *Mi waa dat.* = I want that.   *Mi noh waa dat.* = I don't want that
>
> *Dem goh.* = They went.   *Dem noh goh.* = They don't/didn't go.
>
> Double Negation: *Notn* or *Non*
>
> *Dem du sopm.* They did something.
>
> *Dem noh du notn.* They did nothing. They didn't do anything.
>
> *Dem av sum.*/They have some. *Dem noh av none.*/They have none.
>
> *Dem av.* = They have. *Dem naa(v) non.* = They don't have any.
>
> Standard phonics: *supm*/***sopm***; *sum*/***som***; *dweet*/***dwiit***

Number

Forming Plurals: We form the plural by adding *dem* to the singular noun or by keeping some singular nouns as they are – no change.

A ongl wan kiek yu mek?	Is it only one cake you made?
A nof kiek yu mek?	Did you make many cakes?
Di kiek dem tiess good.	The cakes taste good.
Dash weh di slippaz.	Throw away the slipper (or sandal).
Dash weh di slippaz dem.	Throw away the slippers.
Fling dem weh.	Throw them away.

Mi a fuokos pan di book.   I'm focusing on the book.

Mi a stodi di book dem.   I'm studying the books.

Yu waanta arreenj/arinj?   Do you want an orange? (*waa + a = waanta*)

Yu waa de arreenj dem?   Do you want the oranges?

Yu waa som arreenj?   Do you want some oranges?

Yu waanta slaïs a pier (pear)?   Do you want a slice of avocado?

Yu waa fiuu peess (piis) a pine?   Do you want a few pieces of pineapple?

Eet (iit) a/wan ginep.   Eat a guinep. (Also: *Eet a wan-ginep, noh.*)

Note: "*A wan ginep*" refers to one or just a few. Patwa often treats every noun collectively, but it can treat collective nouns as individual nouns sometimes: *Dem tek out di furnicha dem.* They took out the furniture.

Number and the Body

Body parts are the same in singular as in plural; adding "*dem*" is optional.
Mi bandij mi nii. "I bandaged my knee," or "I bandaged my knees."
Mi bandij mi tuu nee (dem). "I bandaged my two knees."
Di sia-uman look pan di man anmigl.

The seer-woman (palm reader) looked at (read) the man's palm.
Im put katn inna dem tuu nuozwol. "He put cotton in their two nostrils."

Related Vocabulary: *mout*/mouth; *edbak* = back of the head; *edtap*/crown of the head/pate; *ed*/head; *tuo*/toe; *finga*/finger(s); *anmigl*/palm of the hand; *futbatam*/sole(s) of feet; *elbo*/elbow; *an*/hand/arm; *futbak*/calf/heel; *shuolda*/shoulder(s)

Similes in Patwa

Some Patwa similes leave comparison to your imagination:

Di custamma rep fiesty like (kostama rep fiesti laïk)!
"The customer rep is rude like…"

Dem at like wa! (Dem at laïk wa!) They're hot (trendy) like what!

Note: Most similes have immense imagery and use *lakka* ("like") or *noh*.

Nice Similes
Im lov dem like kuk fuud. He loves them like cooked food.

Dem sweet (swiit) lakka sirop.
They're as sweet as syrup (also *"shuga"*/sugar).

Dem dress (jres) noh puss fut.
They're dressed as fancy as a cat's paw.

Dem pitch lakka pichieri. They perch like petchary (birds).

Yu priti like moni. You're as pretty as money (look like a million bucks).

Rough Similes
bad lakka yaaz/as bad as yaws; *krievn lakka aaba shaak*/greedy like harbor-sharks; *a blwoh lakka bull buck*/puffing like bulls (out to gore)

It saaf noh parij (laïk bota). It's as soft as porridge (like butter).

Wi afi bleech/bliich lakka pattu. We had to stay up all night like an owl.

Dem leen an kom een like uol shuuz. They're leaned like old shoes (biased).

Kom een like/"come in like" is common in Patwa; it literally means "is/are just like" (*tof an kom een lakka Afu yam:* tough like Afu yam).

PAAT FWOR

(Part Four)

False Cognates

The English phrase "a while ago" can mean "some time ago," but the same phrase in Patwa suggests "just now" or "very recently" (also "little while": *likl wail*). False cognates sound like your old friends but might be strangers to you. *At times*, English soundalikes are Patwa words with very different meaning. English, the national language, is always there, but Patwa is there even more. Also, don't let pronunciation throw you: *"mats"* means "math." The following list can prevent confusion, but being in a bilingual country, consider the context of your conversation, and -- when unsure – ask for clarity as to whether a word is intended in its English or its Patwa meaning. On a funny note, what sounds like *"Achoo!"* means: "It's true. I agree."

a nex = the next; another (also, *annedda;* regionally: *di nedda*)

aasteerin man = one past the bloom of his youth (**not** "austere in")

again = *(agen)* "Again" can also mean "any longer; no longer" *(naa goh agen* = no longer going).

alto back = halter top; backless crop-top (also, *alta tap* or *altabak*)

an = arm; hand; palm of hand (e.g. He broke his arm: *Im bruk im an.*)

amok = hammock

approach = manners (*Dem naa noh approach.*/They have no manners.)

arreenj = *(adj., noun)* orange (not "arrange")

arm = (*aam*) underarm

bad minded = mean-spirited

batter = *(bata)* struggle to survive (*bata bruuz* = physically abuse; discolored bruise) *batty* = (*vulg.*) buttocks

bizzy = *(bissy/bisi)* kola nut; tea made from the kola nut

bleach = *(bleetch/bliich)* stay up late; lighten skin/hair; clean with bleach

Blouse-an-skirt! = *(blouz an skirt)* a shocked exclamation: *bloü-wow*

blurt naught = *(blert naat)* used as a minced oath

bout = about

box = *(bax)* a very hard slap to the face; angrily slap someone's cheek

brakkish = (describes a drink) not fully sweetened

bright = *(braït)* bright; *bright an fiesty* = impertinent; presumptuous

buck = hit with forehead; stub (one's toe); turn all the way up

buckup = (*bokop*) fluke; *bokop pan/inna* = encounter; collide

bud = **regional** bird; *blakbud* = blackbird (*buddy: vulgar term for* penis)

bully beef = corned beef (has nothing to do with an actual bully)

bungl = *(bongl)* bundle (**not** the English "bungle")

bunks = bounce

bush = very rural area; tea herbs; subsistence farm

chat = talk; gossip

chat peepl = gossip about people; talk behind their back

chuck = (*chuk it*) have an aggressive demeanor; shove someone

cotch = *(katch)* stay at someone else's place without paying (not "catch")

cowl = *(koul)* very cold; freezing weather (*kwol* = moderately cold)

craven = *(krievn)* greedy (*not* cowardly, as in English)

crawny = *(kraani)* nauseating; eliciting scorn; unclean (not "scrawny")

create excitement = *(kriet exaïtment)* make a scene; overreact

crep = *(krep)* canvas tennis shoes

dry eye = (*dry- yai/*"dry-eyed") dry and bold and barefaced; shameless

dung = down (*puddung*: rest something down; *put it dung*: "lay it down")

dungl (-eep) = landfill (not a jungle)

eevlin = evening (It's broken Patwa, not a girl's name.)

eye-water = *(yai waata: baal yaï-waata* = sob*)* tears; "cut-eye": *Im kot im ai.* (He gave a dirty look.)

faass = fast; inquisitive

fall out = *(faal out)* have a disagreement; quarrel; have a breakup

fiesty = rude (**not** English "feisty")

file = foil (as often as "file")

fluxy = *(said of fruit)* of curdled texture due to spoilage

frighten = *(fraï-tn)* fanatical; excitable; giddy in a childish manner

fuss time = *(fos taïm)* in times past; formerly; in the old days ("first time")

glad = glad; naïve/gullible to grab at every lure or be excited by any event

goody = *(inf. slang)* attractive; pretty, good-minded young woman

gorgon = *(gaagan)* informal ruler; bully; one who overpowers others

grievous = *(griivios)* covetous; mean-spirited; vindictive

haughty = *(aati)* healthy

hot word = *(at wod)* rough remarks

hush = *(ush)* "Cheer up, my dear." *("Ush yu mout!"* = "Shut up!")

id = did (*Im id goh.* = "He did go. He went")

I-ya = man (*No, I-ya.* = No, man.)

I'll = What sounds like "I'll" is Patwa "oil." (Standard spelling: *"a- ï -l"*)

jelly = a young coconut; the "meat" inside a young coconut

jockey ride = *(jakki ra-ïd)* piggyback ride

juj = *(joj)* wear daily in domestic life

kaak = *caulk;* cork; (of a venue) filled to capacity

kamikaze = clumsily concocted; makeshift; ill-wrought

knock up = *(nak up)* build haphazardly; put together in a makeshift way

krep = *(crep)* tennis shoes

kunk = strike (with knuckles) on the forehead in reprimand; conch

lass = cutlass (also, *cutliss; mash-yet* = machete)

lay lay = *(liehh-liehh)* idle, waste time

lakka = like or as (not *"lak a":* lack of)

lily/lili = (*regional*) little (*likl*)

long time = years/hours ago (*Mi reech lang taïm*/I arrived hours ago)

long water = *(langwaata)* soup or beverage that is overly dilute

look = *(luk)* pursue amorously; show amorous interest in; look

maass = mask; hide; face-palm; informal/endearing honorific

malice =*(maliss)* give silent treatment to; cut off friendship

marina = merino

masiv = massive; an affectionate address to an audience of any kind

mate = *miet (slang)* the other woman; husband's mistress

meet it = having difficulty (*Dem a meet it.* They're having difficulties.)

mek up = contribute to a purchase; make up (*Im mek up im fies.* = He made a face.)

mine = support; mind; FYI: "It's mine" = *A fi mi* (Patlish: *"Is mines."*)

mine sharp = *(main shaap)* mind you: *If yu noh mine shaap…* If you're not careful…

move = *moov;* behave (*Dem a moov a wieh.* = They're behaving oddly.)

nappy = *(napi)* traditional "bird eye" cloth diaper

nether = *(nedda)* other; *di nedda* or *di nex wan:* "the other" or "the next"

nine-night = (*"nain nait"*) a wake

out = *(v.)* to extinguish; out

owna/uona = owner; (adj.) own: *Im av im uona ous.* He has his own house.

paan = grab a weapon (*Im paan wan pan aŋ fling it:* He grabbed a pan and threw it.)

paashal = biased; merciful (*Dem noh paashal.* They're merciless/unbiased.)

papaa = papaya

pappy shuoh = a laughingstock

peepl = *(piipl)* people; one referring to self (*Im disturb peepl.* He disturbed me.)

picky-picky = *(pikki-pikki)* sparse; (*pik-pik* = to pick at food)

pipe = faucet (or sometimes actually "pipe")

play-play = (*plieh-plieh*) make-believe

pop = *(pap)* break by snapping; dodge someone's pursuit or advances

prime = *(praïm)* insolent beyond one's years (of a child); force-ripe

pop up = *(pap up)* have a fit of laughter

puddung = put down *(pu'dung)* It does not mean pudding/*pudn*.

pull up = disheveled; disrupt; make untidy; bring (a car) to a halt; restart a tune

ram = jampacked; ram

ramp = ramp; play *(fr. Eng.* "romp")

ranking = leader; well-respected man about town

red-eye = envious (like the English green-eyed monster of envy)

response = *(risspanss)* responsible; response

righted = *raïtid*; sane; of sound mind

rung = around; *rung de soh* = around there

runninz = *roninz:* day-to-day happenings (doesn't usually mean run-ins)

rush = accost; attack; chase; hurry; exhilaration; have high demand for

same time = *(siem time)* instantly; immediately; simultaneously

sample = *(sampl)* extraordinarily good, bad or bemusing/amusing

screechy = *(jimskreechih)* sneak up (not making a sound)

shut = "*Shut*" often means shirt, **but** *skirt* is always "skirt" as in English.

sitn = something (does not mean "sitting" – *a siddung* = is sitting)

skiank = traditional reggae dance-steps

skruu = sulk; look sulky; angry expression; a screw for nuts and bolts

skylark = *(skai laak)* to idle

slak = immoral (*slaknis* = carelessness, lewdness)

slobba = *(adj.)* obese (also, *slabba*; does not mean "slobber.")

soap = *(suop)* detergent, dishwashing liquid soap (not TV dramas)

so-soh =*swosoh;* bare; mere; plain; barefaced, only *(*not English "so-so")

spar = *(v.)* hang out together*; (n.)* sidekick (also, *"par"* or *"parrin pee"*)

sport = *(spwut)* sport; take someone partying; go out on the town

strapped-in = *straptin:* heavyset, strapping (also, *trappt-in*)

swat = cram for an exam, study overnight/last-minute

squall = *skwaal, skwaa lih:* pain of hunger and starvation

stunted = *(stontid)* stunned

succumb(s) = *(soh kum)* that's how come; *dass waï*/that's why

swaati = portly (does not mean "swarthy")

swivl = *(swibl)* shrivel; *swibl arinj* = a sour species of orange

tambrin = tamarind (FYI: *tambaree[n]* = tambourine)

tan = (regional) stay; stand; tan

tap = (**rural** speech) stop: *Mi se fi tap di naïz!* = I said to stop the noise.

tek step = exploit (someone) negatively; *tek step a dem* = mistreated them

tek set = harass; *tek set pan (peepl)* = relentlessly pick on (people)

trace = v. (*triess*) argue; quarrel with (n. *triessin*: harsh words)

truss = *(tchoss)* extend credit to; require no up-front payment; trust

ungl = *(ongl)* only (sounds very much like "uncle" – but it's not)

trying = *(tryin)* enterprising; diligent (*a tryin man:* a self-reliant man)

wan = a; one (*Dem av wan nommoh.* = They have only one.)

wine = (*Eng.* wind; Patwa *waïn*) wine; rhythmic motion of waist

what's-it-not = *(watsitnat)* euphemistic swear (not "what-not furniture")

yam = starchy vegetable (**not** sweet potato)

yard = *(yaad)* home; what Jamaicans call Jamaica (*Yaad*)

Idioms

 *Our understanding of these makes conversation a breeze*

A knack for idiom is a secret agent's asset! You get the idiom, because its cultural context isn't lost on you. Patwa relishes idiomatic expression and says some phrases the same way as English or somewhat similarly.

English	Patwa
"might as well"	(same) sounds like: *my tazwel*
"brand name"	*"bran niem"* or *"niem bran"*
"brand new"	*"bran niuu"* or *"niuu bran"*
"is on his Ps and Qs"	*de paŋ im peezaŋkioo (piizankiuu)*
"fly by night"	*fly b'night; pitch b'dieh* (slur: pitch by day)
"to cow a person"	*fi kou dem dong/dung* (to cow them down)
"to curry favor"	*fi korri fieva* (*fi get een wid:* to get in with)
"If I'd (only) known."	*If mi did (ongl) nuo.*
I wasn't born yesterday.	*Mi neva baan yessideh. Mi neva baan big soh.*
"showing true colors"	*Dem shuo dem chuu kolaz.* ("They showed their…")
Pay them no mind.	*Noh pieh dem noh myin. Noh watch dem.*

Many concepts, worded differently, express the same sentiment:

English	Patwa
"Stick a pin."	*Mi noh cut yu.*
"He's in a sticky situation."	*It stikki pan im.*
"That serves you right."	= *"Aggud."*

a "sucker punch" = *naa-luk lik*

a person as a punching bag = *beetin stick (biitn stik)*

That's out of style. = *Dat naa wier*. (Meaning: that's not [being] worn; *naa wier agen* means "no longer being worn." *A uol-taïm sopm*: It's an old-time thing.)

"What came over them?" = *Wa fly inna dem ed? A wa tek dem?*

Don't take that sitting down. = *Miida faït fi dat*. (I'd fight for that.)

"Six of one, half-dozen of the other" is *"six a wan; aaf duzn a di adda"* (or *"siem diffrens"* – literally, "same difference" in English).

The English idiom for being selfishly possessive of something is "to take it to wife"; Patwa modifies that to say "to wife it up."

When English says, "Take your eyes off someone," Patwa says the same thing: *"Tek yu yai aafa dem."* Regarding eyes, Patwa goes further: *yaï-tap* ("eye-top") refers to a precarious position, where if a man blinks, the person on his "eyelid" could fall off. *"Fi liv pan yai-tap"* means "to live at someone's mercy."

Some Patwa prepositions differ, as in: *baal aafta* and *laaf aafta* ("shout at" and "laugh at"). Also, Patwa is *"luk pan"*; the English is "look at."

Gwaan (go on) and *stiehh* (stay) would appear to be opposites, but they say the same thing here: *A soh yu gwaan! A soh yu stiehh! A soh yu apariet.* ("That's how you operate.") *Tan* (regionally, "stand") says it contentiously: *A soh yu tan*.

The word *up* (standard spelling: *"op"*) is in many idiomatic expressions:
"Big up!" = a greeting (sent as a shout-out or given in person) to show respect: *Big up yu self.* Respect to you!
fuul up (fool up) = to trick (also, *"giow"*)
Jim giow uman fi fuul dem up. Jim fibs to women to fool them.

av up = carry grievance
Example: *Noh av dem up.* Don't hold a grudge against them.

fren up: to ingratiate oneself; befriend
Example: *Peepl fren dem up.* People befriend/befriended them.

"Pap up" means "burst into hearty laughter"; to "crack up" into laughter; *"pap dung"* means looking raggedy or falling off.

Pak up = packed; fill; wrap things up, or leave; inveigle.
Example 1: *Pak up!* Finish and get going!
Example 2: *Dem pak up smadi ed.* They filled somebody's head with bias.

Nof up can mean to invite oneself into everyone's space, in a nuisance way.

Full up is "filled": Fill my cup, and let it overflow; fill it up. *Full mi kop, an mek it uovafluo; full it up.*

The word *"ed"* is also in a number of idioms.
Example: *Noh put it pan yu ed.* Don't worry; don't put it on your head. To work one's head/ *"wok"* one's *"ed"* is "to outsmart." Example: *Dem a wok dem ed pan smadi.* = They're fooling someone. (*Wok* has *o* as in *son*)

If your *"ed kwik,"* you're a fast learner. If your *"ed tek yu,"* you went insane.

"Wie" ("way" in English) is also in many idioms:
Wan awie means "by oneself; discreet; discreetly." ("one away")
Im muuv wan awie. He's a loner. He keeps ("moves") to himself.

Im a gwaan a wie, fram dem gaan weh. He's been odd, since they went away. Note: *a wie* ("a way"), *awie* ("away"), and *gaan weh* ("gone away"/migrated). *Gud wiez* means good ways, a good spirit.

Re *"wan"*: *"di wan"* singles someone out. For instance, *"di wan* Clement" is a phrase that singles out "Clement" for unflattering mention.

Popular Phrases

grounz wid = socialize with; establish familiarity with

draa kiaad = deceive; draw card (*draa kiaad pan smadi*: trick someone)

bai out di aagiment = butt in; take over people's dispute (*Eng.* "buy out")

av rubba teet = having rubber teeth; a biteless bark ; no "enforcement"

ex amount = numerous, plenty (also: *ex es amount — from Eng.* excess)

ol brok = hand-me-downs; second-hand clothes (also *wier an lef*)

Plastik sma-il (plastic smile) = fake smile

aass ded an cow fat = cock-and-bull story (Cow ate horse.)

dedlef = bequeathed items

tek set pan = bully; pick on

bun bad lamp = connive; bear ill will

brok di kaana = turn/turned the corner; round the bend; rounded the bend

ketch dem lent = have a field day; enjoy themselves uninhibitedly

weh-it-niem = (*ting-de*) what's-its-name "whatchamacallit"

weh-im-niem-de = what's-his-name

pliess-deh = what's-the-place

chek fi im/ar = to like him/her very much (amorously or otherwise)
chek se = thought; presumed (*Mi chek se yu goh:* "I thought you went.)

kiarriggoh bring kom (kiarigobringkom) = fuel for gossip

dis lang taim (long time) = for a very long while now
evri minit = very frequently ("every minute")

gaan a leed = is/are doing well (*Dem gaan a liid!* They're way ahead!)

naa giim noh gud aagiment = not encouraging him; rejecting his request

tek up fi smadi = take somebody's side; advocate for

get nak = got the short end of the stick

av strent fa = feel bold to challenge

shiem tree ded = have no pride (shame tree died)

*somtaïmish (*English "sometime-ish"*)* = inconstant; blowing hot and cold

plie buoti = straddle the fence; play on both (competing) sides

drap aafa shiepp = failed to maintain

gree wid yu = has a good effect on you (*Dem noh gree*: They don't get on.)

waarbuot = belligerent combative person; bully; contentious, "war-boat"

fon an juok asaïd = "in all seriousness" (fun and joke aside)

luk a food (fuud) = seek to earn one's bread/a day's work/money
eet a food (iit a fuud) = to earn money; *wan bax fuud* (*a* take-out meal)

gladbag = capacity to be joyful (*Dem gladbag bos*: They're overjoyed.)

(if yu noh) maïn shaap = (if you aren't) careful: mind you [literally: mind sharp/sharply]

Complete Idiomatic Statements

Taïm at. The weather is hot. (Time hot. Think "*le temps*" or "*el tiempo*.")

Dem noh gi weh praïaz. They are miserly (give not even a prayer).

Den a ou dem a gallang/gwaan soh? How come they're acting that way?

(Im) a di fos smadi mi si noh niam yam; aaf im life (laïf) gaan.
He's the first person I've seen who doesn't eat yam; half his life is gone.

Dem a noh size (saïz). They are not the same standard/ilk/caliber.

Laad a massi. "Lord have mercy." (Mercy is usually "*mersi*" in Patwa.)

Sopm inna sopm. There's something going on, more than meets the eye.

Dem wol dem kaana. They hold their corner/stay in their place.

Yu nuoh di ting. You know what's up.

But si yah! What a spectacle! ("See here!")

Si wid mi. Bear with me. (Literally, "see with me.")

Every ting korri (curry). Everything's going well.

Dat kaapasset. That's in good stead (*from Eng.* "copacetic").

Yu naa notn fi at yu. You've nothing serious to occupy you.

Yu nuoh wat a clak a stryk? Do you know what's up?
Yu well an nuoh. You well know it.

Kiss mi neck! (Kis mi nek!) What a shock! ("Kiss my neck!")

Dem kiaa mash ants. They're apparently shy and helpless.

Waanti-waanti kiaa geti; Geti-geti noh waanti: Want can't get; *Get* doesn't want.

Kaak yu yez. (Kaak yu iez!) Plug your ears.

Mek mi ier mi yez! Be quiet! (Literally: "Let me hear my ears.")

Dem noh inna it. They want no part (or are not part) of it.

Cut yu ten. (Kot yu ten.) Sit with your legs crossed at the knees.

Dat naa se notn. That's dreary. (Lit.: That's *not* saying *nothing*.)

Daag niam yu sopa. There would be hard consequences. (Dog eats your supper.)

Mi noh yebl fi yu. I have no threshold for your antics.

Waata muor dan flo-wa. It's a sticky situation. (Water's more than flour.)

Mi noh risspanss. I take no ownership of that (not responsible for that).

Noh watch noh fiess. Noh watch notn. Be impartial; pay them no mind. (Don't worry.)
Mi a prie fram mi yai de a mi nee (nii). I've been praying, from I was a child. (From my eyes were at my knees).

Wi spirit tek dem. We like them instinctively (spirit takes them).
Dem waak wid dem belly, noh chuu? They brought a hearty appetite, didn't they?
Dem noh paashal. They're undaunted/merciless; they're impartial.
Dem noh nuo weh niem fried. They know no fear (don't know what's called fear).

Ou yu kum soh? (Ou yu stiehh soh?) Why must you be you like that?
Ress it dong; noh kilop yuself. Put/lay it down; don't hassle yourself.
"Draa dong": "to lose weight or pull down"

"Draa dung pan": "to withdraw funds" or "to approach someone."

Classic Slang

Slang feeds the lexicon of all languages, and Patwa is no different. You hear, *"Oo dem a pruogram?"* in song and conversation. ("Who's their focus?") Much of Patwa slang comes from music, and music from slang.

kleen kleen = admirable, clean, beautiful, pretty, etc.

Taak di tings! = Spill it! Dish!

pree = to focus on

a enz = a hangout spot

tun up = fantastic; exciting; impressive

reddi = (ready) good; done properly

du ruod = be out and about

It sell aaf! = It's great! It's a hit! (Generic meaning: It's sold out.)

a rit aggenss = a grievance being carried (against)

saalt = (adj.) can't catch a break

luk smadi = seek a lover (*smadi*: someone)

wol a fresh = bathe/shower

wol mi kaana = keeping my reserve; remaining in my lane/place

wol a medz = meditate

ress = live or behave

"A de-soh dem ress." That's **where** they live. (Literally: "It's there they rest.")

Note: *"A soh dem ress."* That's **how** they live. ("It's so they rest.")

Lifesaver: Situational Patwa
Ruop een! A Sitiuwieshanal Patwa!
(Rope in! [Enter!] It's Situational Patwa!)

The Jamaican tuck-shop's complement to most rice-and-peas dishes is *vejitebl* ("vegetable"). This is fresh shredded carrots-and-cabbage with no dressing, but many other fresh salads get that same name. At take-outs, you might be asked, "*Yu waant it wid vejitebl aar salad?*" The choice is *vejitebl* or cold macaroni salad. You could be asked, "*Yu waa di axtiel wid fuud?*" *Fuud* is yam, green banana, etc. Tuck shops and roadside stalls, especially in touristy towns, use Patlish -- if not pure Patwa. (Fine dining establishments are entirely different.)

At the Roadside Restaurant

Mi kian get a kaan suup, pleez?
Could I please have some corn soup?

Yu kian get fish tee. It suun dun cook.
You can get fish tea. It'll soon be done.

Yu nuo wa? Mek mi get a kingfish.
Know what? Let me have kingfish.

Yu waant it wid rice *aar wid fuud?*
Do you want it with rice or food?

Ou yu meen? Weh mi se? Mi se, a mi fi tel yu. A mee se fuud!
You know it. What did I say? I said, I'm the one to tell you! It was I who said food. *(*Idiom: *Ou yu miin?* Literally: How/what do you mean?*)*

Lifesaver on the Road

Elp! (Help!)

Luoki: Sum farinna waa elp. Mek wi goh si (a) wa du dem. Waapn to unu? A fuunu kiar dat?
Some foreigners want help. Let's go see what happened to them. What happened to you guys? Is that your car?

Farina: A wi rental. It drap inna patwol; sopm juk de ta-ya, an it poncha.
It's our rental. It fell into a pothole; something pricked the tire, and it got a puncture.

Luoki: Wan ta-ya shap wova de soh -- da Shell de.
A tire shop is over there -- that Shell (station).

Farina: Gud ting it noh lak. Wi wuda miss wi dipaacha taim.
Good thing it isn't closed. We would've missed our departure time.

Luoki: Wi kiaa mek yu miss yu flight, man. (Wi kiaa mek yu mis yu flaït.)
We can't let you miss your flight.

Farina: Nuff rispek. Respect to you. (Rough translation: I appreciate it.)

Shopping (Shopping is fun wholesale or retail *[wolsiel aar ritiel]*.)

Weh yaa sell?	What're you selling?
(A) weh yu waa, mi fren?	What would you like, my friend?
Dem anmied slandaz de.	Those handmade sandals.
Dem ya? Yu laik dem?	These? Do you like them?
Yeh. Dem de. Omoch fi it?	Yes. Those. How much are they?
Ongl sevn gran.	Only seven thousand.
Wa bout da nex wan de?	What about that other pair?
Di uol dem kaas di siem.	They all cost the same.
Mi wi tek di fos wan den.	Then I'll take the first ones.

As You Navigate

Yu laass?	Are you lost?
No. Omoch fi paak ya soh?	No. How much is it to park here?
Tuu bilz a owa.	Two (hundred-dollar) bills per hour.
Weh yu se?	What did you say?
Mi se tuu unjred dala a owa.	I said two hundred dollars an hour.
Gud. Dat sieff.	Good. That's fine ("safe").
Tell mi sopm: Weh yu kom fram?	Tell me something: Where are you from?
Mi kom fram di UK.	I come from the UK.
Omoch a unu?	How many of you?
Mi wan an mi entaia werkpliess.	Me alone and my entire workplace.

Here's more:

Bukstuor av Jumiekan map.	Bookstores have Jamaican maps.
Di bukstwor dem faar?	Are the bookstores far away?
Nat tu dat.	Not very.
Yaago stiet shuo?	Are you going to the stage show?
A wen it staat? Wen it a dun?	When does it start? When does it end?
It staat aredi. It a dun wan a clak.	It already started. It ends at one o'clock.
Wish paat it a keep?	Where is it held?
A yu otel.	At your hotel. ("It's [at] your hotel.")
Mi afi de de! Dat kiaa miss mi!	I'll be there for sure! That can't miss me!
Tek di shukl.	Take the shuttle.

Slice-of-Life Conversation

Di Tipikal Patwa Kanvasieshan (Conversation)

Waa gwaan? Weh yaa du? Yu gud?
What's up? What're you doing? You good?

Yeh, mi a wiet pan a bus (bos). Ou yu du?
Yes, I'm waiting for a bus. How are you?

*Mi gud. Kum ya noh. Ou lang yu out ya? Yu waanta li*f?
I'm good; do come here. How long have you been out here? Want a drive?

Mi out ya bout aaf oua. Di bus suun kom. It de pan di wie, but a lif uda gud still.
I've been out here for about a half-hour. The bus will soon come. It's on its way, but a lift would still be good.

Weh yaago?
Where are you going?

Mi a goh pick up mi kiar a di goraaj.
I'm going to pick up my car at the garage.

Kom wi goh, den noh! Put yu bag inna di trunk.
Let's go (then)! Put your bag in the trunk.

Aatomuotiv Vokabuleri (Auto Vocabulary)

kiar = car   ***spier paat*** = spare parts   ***aato paat*** = auto parts

winsheel = screen   ***duor angl*** = door handle.   ***winda*** = window

ud = bonnet   ***agzelarieta*** = accelerator   ***brieks*** = brakes

muota = motor   ***injin*** = engine   ***gias pedal*** = gas pedal

Gias sel bai di leeta. Gas is sold by the liter (*liita*).

Conversation Two

Waapn, sah? Waa gwaan?
What's up, man? What's going on? ("*Sah" is an informal/friendly* "sir.")

Notn naa gwaan. Mi de ya. Ou yu du? Weh yu up tu?
Nothing's going on. I'm here. How are you? What're you up to?

Mi a map out a bizniz fi mi self inna di diehh ya.
I'm mapping out a business for myself on this day ("in the day here").

Wa kyna bizniz? A waddat? A wa dem de yaa uol up? (Wa kaïna...)
What kind of business? What's that? What are those you're holding up?

Som baatsuut pitcha. Yu laïk dem? Mi mek baatsuut. Mi waa sell dem.
Some swimsuit pictures. You like them? I make swimsuits. I want to sell them.

Yeh! Wan pliess de de fi elp yu. Seet de (si it de). Yu nuoh wish paat dat?
Yes! A place is there to help you. There it is. Do you know which place (part) that is?

Yeh:.SBA - Smaal Bizniz. A de soh mi fi goh, noh chuu? Miebi mi goh.
Yeah, SBA – Small Business. That's where I should go, isn't it? Maybe I'll go.

Yu sieff, man; sekl yu self. Kaal dem bout bizniz inkiubieta an dem sopm de. A dat yu fi du.
You're in good shape; don't pressure yourself. Call them about business incubators and those things. That's what you should do.

Yeh man. Tanks fi di info. Rispek! Yes. Thanks for the info. Respect to you.

Rasta Patwa

Rasta, early Reggae ambassador, lifts the dignity of the African Diaspora and all the world. In *The Rastafarians*[7] Leonard E. Barrett Sr. notes that Rasta's contribution to Patwa has been in effect "since the 1950s" (Barrett, p.5). Rasta Patwa is as strong as ever! *I-ts, green, and guol!* *(Ites = red)*

Conversation

Yes, I! Waapn, king? Bless up yuself!	What's up, friend? Be blessed.
Waapm, mi bredda?	What's up, brother?
Mi jos a wol a medz. Waa gwaan, I-ya?	Just meditating. What's going on?
I-man a faawod, zeen?	I'm leaving (coming/going), see?
I a faawod tu. Yu noh zeet?	Me too. Get what I'm saying?
I-ri noh. Eezy noh, mi bredrin.	Take it easy, friend (**or** *I-drin*).
Empress, rispek, sistrin! Blessed love!	Hi, my sister; respect to you!
Mek wi riizn; tell I di roninz.	Let's reason; tell me what's up.

Phrases

Irie = (I-ri) good, pleasant, mellow

upful yuut = upstanding lad

roninz (runninz) = happenings

Fa-ya (faïa!) bun! Bun a fa-ya pan dat! = Rebuke that. Burn a fire on that.

(Yu) zi mi? = Do you understand me (i.e., understand what I'm saying)?

---

[7] *The Rastafarians: Twentieth Anniversary Edition*, Beacon Press, 1997

Appreciating the Vein of Rasta Patwa

No "*ded*" only "live": dedicate = *livicate/livikieshan*

No underdog, only over: understand = *ovastan*

Never the "end" of joy' only the "full" of joy: enjoy = *fulljaai*

No iet (no hate) -- not 'ating anyone: appreciate = *appreeshilov*

Jehovah = *Jah* or *Jah-Jah*   Jah knows! = *Jah nuoh! Jah-Jah nuoh!*

natrality = *I-tal;* natural; in food: no-sodium; in lifestyle: organic

Babylon = *babilan:* vanity; materialism; imperialism

Rasta Patwa usually has no first-person object pronoun. You won't hear "mi" in undiluted Rasta Patwa, only "*I*" or "*I an I.*"

Example: "*I teech dem, an dem teech I.*" (Regular Patwa: *Mi tiich dem.*)

"Someone" is *"a wan."* People can be *"wans an wans."*

Isn't that what I'm telling you/him? *"Den noh dat I a shuo a wan?"*

When preceded by *"di,"* the "*I*" can mean "you."

Example: *Weh di I a goh?* "Where are you going?"

Soh weh di I-dem a se? = "What are you saying?" (This is "What's up?" The *"soh"* is a filler. *"Di I"* is singular; *"di I-dem"* is plural.)

"I" can replace prefixes: *I-ditiet* (meditate), *Inity* (unity), *Itinually* (continually)

Rasta "*I*" can also mean "my": *I daata goh a maakit fi goh get bresheh an I-lalluu.* My girl goes/went to the market to get breadfruit and callaloo.

PAAT FAIV

(Part Five)

Patwa-English Vocabulary

(Abbreviations: n/noun; v/verb; s/singular; pl/plural; colloq/colloquial; inf/informal; pej/pejorative; reg/regional; sl/slang; vulg/vulgar)

a = a; am/is/are *(Dem fi av a aat.* = They should have a heart.)

A wa? = What is it?

a^2 = to; at *(Mi a goh a wan paaty.* = I am going to a party.)

a^3 = *conversation filler*: *A waagwaan?* What's going on?

a^4 = *(reg.)* have *(regional: Dem naa non.* = They don't have any.)

aaba = harbor

aad yez = *(aad iez)* stubborn; willful

aada yerin = *(aada ierin)* hard of hearing

aaf = off; half

aal = all; haul *(aal now* = even now; up to now; even until now)

aala = all of

aalanpul = *(aal an pul)* manhandle *(Eng.* "haul and pull")

aanda = under

aanda mannaz = under reprimand/rule; under close supervision

aass = horse *(aas*; *jakaas* = jackass)

aarait = alright; *(inf.* "Hi!")

aatikal = authentic

"*A behh*" is a childhood taunt. *Abbe-seed* is a small fruit.

abeng = Maroon horn

afi = have to (*Mi afi goh.* I have to go. *Yu naafi goh.* You don't have to go.)

Afu yam = yellow yam (**not** sweet yam or sweet potato)

ag = pig; pigs ("hog")

agen = again; any longer; no longer: *Mi naa goh agen*/I'm no longer going.

ahwoh = *(a wuo: emphatic filler to imply threat)* You better!

aï = *eye* (also *yai; yaï-waata* = tears)

aïgl = *(I-gl)* idle

ak = act

akl = manhandle; to hassle, manipulate; stress out someone (n., *aklin*)

akshan = action

Aktchwali = *(akchuali:* **high-context** *hyperbole for "nearly")* actually

alibotn = gullible worker; unpaid laborer; exploited volunteer

Anansi = shrewd spider of local lore or anyone like him (*etym.* Akan: spider)

an = arm, hand (*fwol dem an:* fold/folded their arms)

anbag = handbag

andastan = understand

apparieshan = *(aparieshan)* operation

appariet = *(apariet)* operate

astrieh = astray

at wud = *(at wod; regional)* hurtful remarks; cruel comments

atta = hotter *(Regional: Atta mi noh gat i'. After all, I don't have it.)*

attaklaps = catastrophe with drama/excitement (Patlish: *hattaclap*)

baachoom = *(baachuum)* bathroom

baanlan = the land of one's birth

baaskit = basket

bad = bad; badly () *bad-bad* = extremely *jelos bad-bad*

bada = worse/*wos*; bother (e.g., *Mi kiaa bada:* I can't bother.)

badwud = *(badwod)* profanity

bafan = clumsy

bagij = baggage

bag waïa = *(bag wa ya)* barbed wire

baggass bwud = *(bagas buod)* bagasse board

bak = back; support; draw a weapon (*Im bak im ratchit.* He drew his blade.)

bak-ansa = backtalk (also, *bak-chat*)

bakfut = hind leg

bakkittiv = *(bakitiv)* support, backing

bakl = bottle; battle

ban = band; ban; bandage (*girt di wies* = gird waist; *ban yu belly* = mourn)

bandaana = traditional Madras plaid fabric used for Jamaican national costume

bandoolu = *(banduulu)* bootleg; under-the-table; illicit; black market

bandy leg = *(bandileg)* bow-legged stance (*nak nee* = knock-kneed)

barroh = *(baro)* borrow; wheelbarrow

batta = struggling (*Dem a batta/bata.* = They're struggling.)

battabrooz = *(batabruuz)* physically abuse; discolored bruises

beess = *(biis)* beast

beez = bee; bees (e.g., *Mi si wan beez/biiz*: I see a bee.)

beg-beg = always begging

ben/wenna = (**regional** aux verb) *Mi ben goh/wenna goh*: I went/was going.

berrial = *(berial)* burial

bess = *(bes)* best

bier = *(beer)* bear; beer; bare

bifwor time = *(bifuor taim)* prematurely

big up = laud; give recognition to

bih = *(bi)* be (*fi bi* = to be)

bikkaa =*(bikaa)* because

Binghi = (pronounced *bing gih*) Niyabinghi Rasta

bingi = (rhymes with Eng. "dinghy") slingshot

blai = *(bly)* lenience; favor ("*Gimi a blai.*" = "Be lenient/kind.")

bleech = stay up late; stay awake all night; lighten the skin; bleach

bless = bless (*"Blessed!"* = Rasta greeting)

blytid = *(blai tid)* spoilt; undermined

Bobo = Bobo Rasta

bokop = fluke; unexpected success

bongo = dreadlocks; drum

boogooyagga = *(bugu yaga)* crude; makeshift

boogu = *(bugu)* dried snot

bou = bow; bough

bout = about; a set in a match, etc.

braata = bonus (popularly spelt: *brawta*)

braatupsi = home training; decorum

bredda = *(breda)* brother (regionally: *brabbrah*)

brekfruut = *(regional)* breadfruit

briid = get pregnant (inf. *Shi a briid.* = She's pregnant. "*Shi a*" is pronounced *shia*. Very pejorative and informal: *Im briid ar.* He got her pregnant.)

bringl = be annoyed; to bristle

brok = (v.) break: *It wi brok.* = It will break. (The noun "break" is *briek*.)

bulla = sweet round cake made with ginger/coconut; *(colloq.)* sharp rebuke

bumshuss = *(bomshos)* bumptious

bun = *(bon)* bun; burn; infidelity (*bun-bun* = dinner-pot scrapings)

bu-nu-nu-nus = delightful

bus up = *(bosop)* destroyed; broken up, burst

bus = *(bos)* get fame; tattle; burst; bus; hit a glycogen wall; run out of stamina

bush jakit = bush jacket: semi-formal shirt worn outside trousers

butu =*(derogatory)* hooligan; *baxbout butu* = itinerant hooligan

bwaai = boy

bwaai-ō bwaai = expression of bemusement or frustration

bwonify = (*buonifai*) *slang: bona fide*; genuine

bwonos = bonus; *braata*

bwosi = *(buosi)* fancy; flashy; showy; disdainfully showing off

bwud man = *(buodman)* empty-headed, unfeeling man

bwun = *(buon)* bone

chaa = *(regional)* chew; *chaa-chaa-up* = chewed up

chaaja = charger

chaaklit = chocolate

chaka-chaka = haphazard; untidy; disorganized

chap = chop; wound with a cutlass/machete

chaparita = heavy bracelet

chat-chat = babbling; gossiping

chek fa = to like (also *chek fi*)

Cho! = expression of humor or annoyance (*chuocho* = a squash vegetable)

chok = shove someone (*chok badniss* = act a bully; *chok aaf* = to dive)

chubl = *(chobl)* pick on; mess with: *Noh chubl dem.* = Don't mess with them.

chuu = true; chew; through (*chuudat/*"because of that"

chuu stik = chewstick)

chuo = *(chuoh)* = throw; *chuo wud* = make veiled assertions

chuppidniss = *(chupidnis)* stupidity; nonsense

chups = little platonic kiss: peck on the cheek

crabtoh = (*krabtuo/kraptuo*) illegible handwriting

cry-cry = (also: *krai krai* [*Eng.* "cry"]) emotional; always tearful; whiny

da… de = that (*da wan de* = that one)

da… ya = this; (*da wan ya* = this one)

daag = dog

daagaat = cruel; heartless person (also *daagaattid* [*adj.*])

daata = daughter

danjuz = dandruff

dankilents = win by many lengths (*Eng.* "donkey's lengths")

das = *very popular Patlish phrasing* of "that's" (*Das wai.* = That's why.)

dashiki = African-style tunic shirt

dash-weh = *(dashwe)* spill/spilt; thrown away; abort; dismiss; discard

deggeh deggeh = (*dege dege*) only: *wan deggeh-deggeh wan* = only one

deh = to be part of an unmarried couple

de de = is/are there (*Dem [noh] de de.* = They're [not] there.)

dem… de = those (*dem dish de* = those dishes)

dem… ya = these (*dem dish ya* = these dishes)

diam = damn (*dam* = *dam*)

didda = *(aux. verb: did a)* was/were: *Yu didda sleep?* Were you sleeping?

dieda dieh = the other day

dieh = day (*a dieh time* = in the day; during the days)

dienja-russ = *(dienjaros)* dangerous

difrent = different; (*idiom*) having a mutual understanding

Dinki Mini = ancestral dance to cheer wakes; nine-night dance ritual

dippenn = *(dipen)* depend; depend on = *dippenn pan*

dongruo = *(inf.)* having stunted physical growth

doonduss = *(dundus) pej.* albino

drunkad = *(dronkad)* drunkard; alcoholic

du = do (*Noh du wi dat*: Don't do that to us. *Wi neva du yu notn*: We didn't do/never did anything to you. *Noh du wi notn*. Don't do anything to us. *Dem du dem sopm*: They did their thing/something to them. *Dem du sopm fi dem.* = They did something for them.)

dun = *(don)*) already; finish; *Yu dun nuo*: "You already know."

dunk-ya = careless; reckless; uncaring (*Dem donk-ya.* = They're irresponsible.)

dunt = Isn't it? Aren't they? Do you agree/think so? (also, *dwunt, dont, dwo*)

duppy = *(dopi)* ghost

dweet = *(dwiit)* do a thing; get something done; achieved something

dwoh = though (To avoid ambiguity, this book doesn't spell it "duo" as standard.)

edtap = pate (i.e., crown of the head)

eed = (*iid*) heed; *tek iid* = take heed: *Tek eed!* Take heed!

eediat = (*iidiat*) idiot

een = (*iin; inna*) in

egzop = pushy

elboh = *(elbo)* elbow

ennop = ended up (*Dem enop lef.* = They ended up leaving.)

enka = hanker

extra = spare; excess (*extranniss* = uncalled-for behavior)

faada = father (or greeting showing respect: *"Yes, faada! Yes, dads!"*)

Faahwod! = Encore!

faak = fork

faass = fast; tamper; nosy; *faasniss* = curiosity; nosiness; inquisitiveness

faktchrih = *(fakchri)* factory

fambilly = *(fambili)* family

farinna = *(farina)* foreigner

fee miel = *(fiimiel)* female

feelinz = *(fiilinz)* feelings (*kiar*/carry *feelinz* = hold grievance; *feel it fi* = feel for)

fenke-fenke = puny (*"fe ne"* **or** *"fe ne griis"* = battle serious difficulties)

furnicha = *(fernicha)* furniture

fiek = fake

fiess = face (*fies bwaai* = handsome guy ["face boy"])

fiesty = *(fiesti)* sassy; disrespectful; rude; presumptuous

fieva = favor; resemble; a courtesy or help; a good deed; friendly help

fievrit = favorite

fingl fingl = touch excessively

finna ral = *(finaral)* funeral

fitteeg = *(fitiig)* fatigue; exasperate

fitteeg-in = *(fitiigin)* tiresome

fluxy = *(floxi)* of infirm texture

fond = fond

foo-fool/fufuul = very foolish; fool-fool

foolinnish = stupidity; nonsense

foot = *(fut)* shin; foot [every lower part of leg]

footbaal = *(futbaal)* soccer

frak = conservative gown/dress

fraktiel = hem of dress/skirt

frowzy = exuding damp/stale/sweaty smell

full = *(v., n., adj., adv.)* fill; full

fun = *(fon)* fund; fun

futbak = calves *(regionally:* heel)

fwoss = *(fuos)* force; *fwoss ripe* = rude to grownups; disrespecting elders

fwun = *(fuon)* phone

galang = misbehave, carry on; go; *(imperative)* Leave!

gial = *(inf. or pej.)* gal, girl *(gial-iss* = womanizer; philanderer; ladies' man)

gianzi = guernsey; men's casual buttonless pullover; t-shirt

giarrisn = politically partisan neighborhood; violently partisan area

giim = *(gi im)* give it to him (Patwa only has hard *g* as in English "get.")

ginigag = head cook and bottle washer; leader of it all

gizzaada = coconut candy

giow = *(giou)* pull a prank; trick someone by way of a fib

gravalishos = greedy (*grah -vah - lish – us*)

gree = *(grii)* get along together; agree (*Dem noh gree.*/They don't get along.)

grieta = grate; grater; greater

grojful = envious; jealous (*grojfulniss* = envy)

grung = ground; a person's own subsistence farm (where food is grown)

gud an prapa = very well (good and proper)

gudda = might have (*Dem gudda dweet.* They might do it.)

guodi = calabash; gourd

gwaan = *(guaan)* run along; go on; continue

gwain = going; going to (do something)

gweh = *(gu weh)* Get lost! Go away! (Also: *Klier aaf! Clear off!*)

ignarant = ignorant *(ignaranss* = ignorance)

iida = either

imij (im-ij) = images; imagery; persona

innoh = *(conversation filler, ino)* you know

innof = *(inof) sufficient (A noh inof:* It isn't enough. *It inof:* It's enough.*)*

insipid = insipid

inspaïa = inspire

I-rih = good and pleasant (traditional popular spelling: *irie*) *irrizzistebl* = irresistible

issy = *(issi)* you see

istri = history

jaa = cheek; jaw *(kiss ar pan ar jaa* = kissed her cheek)

jaabuon = jawbone

Jan Poblik = (*eni an evribadi:* any and everyone) the public

jenda = gender

jerraaf = giraffe

jingbang = (*pej.*) children thrown about; jalopy

jinji = large fly

jinnal = trickster (*"jinal"*: also spelt *"ginnal"*)

jankunu = costumed folk characters from John Canoe/"Jonkanoo"

juk = poke; pierce something

junjo = *(jonjo)* fungus; moss

juok = joke (*juokifai* = having a sense of humor "jokify")

juu = due; dew

kaatan = cardboard box

kaapariet = cooperate

kabba-kabba = *(kaba-kaba)* knocked together; makeshift; disorganized

kabbla = inept one (*Dem a kabla:* They have no expertise but shoddy work.)

kallah up = grab a man by draping his clothing (also, *driep up*)

kanfrenss = *(kanfrens)* conference

kan-nyvin = *(kanaïvin)* conniving

karaachi = karate

kass-kass = hearsay; contention

katch = *(kach)* stay on at someone's home; precariously place an object

katta = *(catta)* cloth that cushions weight carried on one's head

kaya = dried coconut husk; coir

ketch/kiatch = catch (*ketch up* = reach alongside; get up-to-date; quarrel)

kette = (of music) *Kete* drum

kiaad = card

kiaat = cart; *ankiaat* = handcart

kiamra = camera (also *kiamma-ra*)

kiaŋ = can (*kiaa/kiaaŋ* = can't)

kiaa = can't be (*It kiaa shier*: It can't be shared.)

kiangl = candle

kiar = *(kiarr)* car; carry (*kiar batchri* = car battery)

kiarrat = carrot; karat

kiash = cash

kiaasl = *(kiasl)* castle

kiat = cat

Kiattalik = Catholic; *(regional)* catalytic

kibba = be quiet; *Kibba yu mout!* = Be quiet! *kibba aatbun* = cover heartache; cover figurative "heartburn")

kieh-ta/kieta = care (*Mi noh kieh-ta.* = I don't care.)

kielliss = *(kielis)* careless

kiepebl = capable

kimboh = akimbo

kin teet = laugh (also, *skin teet*)

kip = *(mostly regional)* keep

kiss yu teet = hiss your teeth

klaafi = (also, *claffy*) clumsy person; simpleton

klaat = *(claat)* suffix of explicit swear words; cloth

kliem = claim

kly-din = (*klaïdn*) cloying: *Mi kly'da it.* = I'm cloyed of it.

kom = come (also a filler: *kom tel* = told; *kom mek* = made)

kom wi… = *let us… let's…*

komplien = complain; complaint

koob = chicken coop

koro bunkos = carbuncle

korouchiz = junk; clutter

kraa (up) = rip someone's skin with one's fingernails *(kraab)*

kraasiz = problems; worries

krabbit = aggressive; having a cruel nature

kratchiz = *(kra-chiz)* crotch; slang slur referring to a covertly hostile person

krebbeh = *(krebe)* slob; crass person with no home training

kriet = create

krievn = greedy

kritchol = screech owl

kruff = *(krof)* oaf; hoodlum; *krufty* = burdensome (also, *"Kunu-munu"*)

krumuujin = miserly; selfish *(from Eng. "curmudgeon")*

ku (de) = look (there), Also *ku ya*: look here; *ku pan…* = *(derog.)* look at…

kudn = couldn't

kulcha = *(kolcha)* culture; *kulcharal/kolcharal* = cultural

kumbullo = *(regional)* shady clique

Kumina = Afro-Jamaican religion and its dance

kunu munu = hooligans

kuol = cold (*chaa kwol* = charcoal)

kwaaril = quarrel

kwaata = quarter

kwabz = *(s/pl)* close crony; co-conspirators; close accomplices

kwaiat = *(kwa-yat)* quiet

kwente = personal business (*Myin yu wona kwente.* = Mind your own business.)

kwint = blink

kwoss = *(kuos)* coarse, course (*kwoss up* = handle roughly)

laaks = minced oath (Lord!)

laan = lawn; outdoor dancehall venue

labrish = *(verb/noun)* gossip

ladda = ladder

laiad (la-yad) = liar

liiv = time off from work *(taim aaf fram werk)*

lan = *(verb/noun)* land; LAN

leg = *(human)* thigh; fast-food chicken "drumstick"

leggo = let go; *leggo beess* = *(legobiis)* a brawler; rowdy people

libati = liberty; liberties *(fi tek libati wid smadi* = to take liberties with someone)

lieh wiet =*(liewiet)* waylay; FYI: to lie down is *"lieh dung"* or *"liddung"*

lik = hit; slap; lick

likki-likki = *(liki liki)* greedy; corruptible

likl = little; *likl-likl* = little by little; *very* little

listong = lisp

luggoh-luggoh = *(logologo)* haul; carry *(Eng.* "lug")

lugz rih = *(logzri)* luxury

luk (look) = look; pursue amorously *(look pan* = look at; *look fa* = look for)

luoftaz = idlers who loaf *(luof aafa; spunj pan* = sponge off others)

maabl = marbles; marble

maaga = meager; skinny

maakup = defaced; scarred

maal = marl; mall

maama man = gossipy, quarrelsome man *(derived from: maama/*murmur)

maanin = morning *(a maanin/*in the morning; *"a maanin time"/*every morning)

maass = *(rural courtesy)* sir: *Maass Taam* = Sir Tom

maka = *(popularly: macca)* thorn

madda = mother

magl = model

maliss = *(malis)* give silent treatment to; cut off a friendship with

mash-up = *(mashop)* ruin; crushed; undermine

mashietid = dilapidated

maskitta = mosquito

maskut = mascot

matta = dried mucus from the eyes

mattee-ral = *(matiirial)* material

meeda = *(miida)* I was in the process of… (Reg.: *"miina" or "mi enna"*)

mek = *(v.)* let; make; allow; force

mek wi… = let's… (also *"kom wi"*: *Kom wi goh waak.* = Let's take a walk.)

mellan = *(melan)* watermelon

memba = member; remember: *Mi (noh) memba.* = I (don't) remember.

miebi = *(mieh-bih)* maybe

miel = male; mail

miit = meat; meet (*miit iina aksident* = met with an accident/collision)

mikkiess = hurry; get a move on (*Eng.* "make haste")

Missa = Mr. (*mista* is common noun "mister")

mistiek = error; mistake

mizza rebl = *(mizarebl)* miserable

mout a massy = *(mouta massi)* a gossip; chatterbox

mowly = moldy; stale/damp smell

musmus = *(regional)* mongoose

mussi = *(mosi)* probably; speculative: must be

naa = not *(Mi naa ramp.* = I'm not playing.) Regionally: doesn't have

nashinnal = *(nashinal)* national

nat up = *(nat op)* tangled

neh-in = *(regional)* didn't *(noh-ehn/nen*; e.g., *Mi nen goh.*/I didn't go.)

nekbak = nape

nengeh-nengeh = (pronounced *"neng eh neng eh"*) nag; pester; whine

niam = (*v.* also, *eet*) eat (often spelt '*nyam*' in Patwa)

niebl = navel (*niebl string* = umbilical cord)

niebl arrinj = navel orange(s)

nieh shan = *(nieshan)* nation

noh = don't; doesn't (*Mi noh nuoh*: I don't know. *Noh dweet*: Don't do it)

Noh choo? = *(Nochuu?)* Don't you think so? Isn't that so? Isn't that true?

*noh*² = (filler of coaxing or courtesy) *Kom noh.* = Do come. *Du noh.* = Do.

nof = *(nuff; nof nof)* abundant; plenty; ever-present

nuoh = *(nuo)* no; know

nuoznaat = snot

oudi duu = howdy; a hello

olsta stomok = stomach ulcer

ongl = only

oudi = *(very rural)* How do you do?

outta aada = rude; offensive (*Eng.* "out of order")

paadna = partner; informal savings group with community banker

paadna draa = each *paadna* member's total-savings payout

paarin paadna = sidekick; friend with whom one goes everywhere

paass = *(paas)* pass; *di paass* = the past

paass yu place = overstep your bounds

palaav = (also, *pal aaf*) sprawl oneself; recline; show off

pan = on; pan

pap = pop; break sharply; nimbly dodge

pap stuori = gossip (also *"labrish"*)

par = *(n.* also, *spar)* sidekick; par = *(v.)* hang out with; par

parraps = *(paraps)* perhaps

patty = popular meat-filled pastry

patu = owl (pronounced "pattu")

patwaata = broth leftover from boiling food

patwol = *(patuol)* pothole

peessn = *(piisn)* put together (A *peess* is also land: cane-piece/*kienpiis*.)

piaa piaa = paltry, weak, ineffectual

pier = avocado pear; pier/jetty; pure

pieza = store curb *(from Italian "piazza")*

pig = pig; pigs (*ag* = hog)

pikni = child (also, *pikinni; very informal, often offensive*)

plat = plait; plot

plieh plieh = *(plie-plie)* make-believe

poco = *(poh koh)* African-Jamaican religion *(jump poco* = to dance *poco)*

praïaz = *(pry-yaz)* prayer; prayers

pranganat = pomegranate

pree = (*slang*) observe; concentrate on

prekkeh = fool

pritti-pritti = *(priti priti)* colorfully decorated

prizomshoss = presumptuous

pull-up = in disarray *(pull up* = put something in disarray; restart a song)

puncha = puncture

ponkin = pumpkin

putus = dear one; darling

raatid = *(interjection)* dang; minced version of expletive *raass*

raa-chaa = plain; rough; undiluted; unceremonious

ram sak = ransack

red Ibo = (**pejorative**, also *reddibbo* or *doondooss/dundus*) albino

renk = rank smell; presumptuous; rude

riakshan = reaction

riddim = rhythm; drum-and-bass; instrumental

riess = race (slang: *riess up* = reprimand; *riess dem up* = reprimand them)

riettinz = high regard (*Dem nuh gi im nuh riettinz.*/They don't rate him highly.)

rispek = respect

rizziss = *(rizis)* resist

rubba = *(roba)* pencil eraser

run dung = chase; *rondong* = coconut gravy for fish (like Asian "rendang")

ron kom = come quickly; do eagerly (*Im ron kom tek it:* He took it eagerly.)

saada = solder; weld

saaf = soft (*saafaz/saps* = timid person)

sah = sir; friendly address to a man

samfai = tricky

saampl = remarkable or perplexing person or thing

sangwij = sandwich

sanky = dirge

saïans = *(sa-yanss)* science; sorcery

se fe = This means: "Dare me."

sekl = become calm; settle

sell = sell; sold

serva = (computer) server

setaan = stealthy matchmaker; instigator

sheggry = foolishness (*sheg up* = selfish; [n] destroy; *sheg wid* = mess with)

shiep = shape; person's figure (*shiepp aafa* = feign a strike at) *shub out* = protrude; venture out; launch

shuoh = movie; concert; stage show; *(v.)* to show; exhibit

sick = sick (*siki siki* = sickly; frequently ill)

siddung = *(sidong)* sit

sieff = safe; *colloq.* "in good stead"

siekka = due to; because of (*Eng.* "for the sake of")

sitn = something (also, *sopm*)

skellian = scallion

skenggeh = reggae strum

skip = cut ahead of those in a queue; skip

skrapsiz = (*krapsiz*) remnants of material; piece of scrap; scraps

skrimij = street soccer; any-number-a-side football (*Eng.* "scrimmage")

skull = *(skol)* be truant; skull; *skull skuul* = be truant from school

skwinj (up) = *(skuinjop)* make small; shrink oneself

sky juice = *(skaï juus)* "street-food" drink: cane syrup/shear-ice/water in bag

sky laak = *(skaïlaak)* to idle

slakniss = *(slaknis)* vulgarity; lewd lyrics; carelessness

smadi = *(smaddy)* somebody

soh langss = *(solangs)* so long as; as long as

soh til = *(sotil)* until; as an intensifier: *Im api soh til.* = He's exceedingly happy.

son = son; sun

soun = sound; sounds; soundly *(e.g., sleep soun)*

spar = friend (derived with opposite meaning from *Eng.* "sparring partner")

spwyil = (*spwaïl* [rhymes with English "style"]) spoil; spoilt

stanop = *(v.) stand*

stieshan = *(stieh shan)* station; police station

streggeh = *(stre-ge)* uncouth person

strieh = *(strie)* stray; *strieh weh* = *(v.)* stray; go astray

stucky = *(stoki)* short and stocky; children's game (similar to "tag")

stush = uppity; discerning; pretentious

supm or *sitn* = (*sopm/sopn* or *sinting*) something

su-su = *(suss/sussu/se se)* gossip

sweety = *(swiiti)* candy

swoja = *(suoja* [informal: *swoji*]) soldier

swoja klaïm = (soldier climb) a boost, getting a leg up to scale a wall

swol = soul (*swolz* = afro hair; soul music)

taak = talk; referring: *A oo yaa taak?* To whom are you referring?

tablit = tablet

tallawa = *(talawa)* resourceful

tambrin = tamarind

tandeh = wait (*tan de:* from *Eng.* "stand there")

tapanaris = *(tappa-naa-riss)* boastful snob

tchrang = *(regional)* strong

teef = *(tiif)* thieve; *(s/pl)* thief

teggerreg = war-boat person; cantankerous personality

tek = take (*tek up fi* = take someone's side)

tek...mek = turn... into (*tek it mek* = turn it into)

tek-set pan = stalk; relentlessly bully

tell... aaf = speak harshly to (*tell dem aaf* = scold them ["tell them off"])

Tenki. = *(very rural)* Thank you.

ting = thing; *di ting* = the trend/"in" thing (You know what's up: *Yu nuo di ting*.)

ting de = what's-its-name (also, *weh-it-niem-de*)

tochiz = *(tutchiz)* easily upset; touchy; loves to touch

trouziz = *(trowziz)* trousers

tump =*(tomp)* punch, hit with closed fist (*tumpa* = short and stocky)

tun = turn (*tun kaanmeel* = a dish like Italy's *polenta*)

tun up = *[sl.]* great

tups = a tiny bit; very small amount

twoh =*(tuo)* carry someone on the crossbar of a bicycle

ummutch = *(omoch)* how much (How much?)

unkop = (often spelt: *oonkup*) stuffed together; crammed into small space

uu = who (*Uu sen yu [kom]*? Who sent you? *Dem sen im*: They sent him.)

uufa = Whose? (*A uu an dem?* = Who's [in it] with them?)

verjan = version; instrumentals side of a song; type of

waak gud: walk/travel safely; *waak dem out*: step away to avoid argument

waakbout: having a love of wandering (the streets)

Waapn? = What's happening? (also, *Waapm?*)

waata = water

wagga-wagga = unkempt; excessive

wala = wallow

weh = where; (*wa*) what; *wa dieh/weh dieh/fram wa dieh* = recently

Weh fi du? = What to do? (What is one to do [about something]?)

weh it niem (deh) = what's-it-called; what-you-may-call-it

wen = when

weskut = men's suit-vest; waistcoat

wi = we; will; our (*Wi paak wi kiar.* = We parked our car.)

wiet = wait (Patwa *wiet* sounds like English "yet" with a "w" in front.)

woleep = plenty (*woleepa kluoz* = plenty clothes; also, *nof*)

woleeppa = vast amount of; also, *uoliip* **or** *nof*

wok = work; "werk": *Im de a werk.* He's at his job. (*woklis* = worthless)

wōm = *(uōm)* home

uopn bak = reopen; backless dress/blouse (*uopn-bak van* = pickup truck)

yaa = (conversation filler/softener) y'hear

yabba = clay pot ("*labba*" or "*yabba yu mout*" = prattle; tattle)

yamil = where yam is grown

yetrij = hatred

yezring = earring (also, *ehring; iezring*)

yuut = *(yoot)* young man; young people collectively

English-Patwa Vocabulary

a = (article) *a, wan*

a² = has; have

a³ = it is; there is; conversation filler; auxiliary verb in the continuous tense

about = *boh, bout* (also pronounced *"bow"*)

accoutrement = kutchument

active = *aktiv* (pronounced exactly as in English)

adore = *adwor (aduor)*

after = *afta; aafta*

again = *aggen (agen)*

agent = *iejent* (Remember: the Patwa *"i"* is *short* as in "dip.")

amaze = *amiez (am-yez)*

another = *annedda; a nex wan*

answer = *ansa*

anymore = *noh muor* (*any = noh*: *mi noh niid noh..* I don't need any...)

anything = *eniting*; *notn* (I didn't say anything: *Mi neva se notn.*)

anyway: *enny-wie (eniwie)*

anywhere = *enny-weh (eniwe); noh matta wish paat*

arrange = *arienj*

arrival = *(araïval)* arrival

arrive = *reech [alt. spelling: riitch], arrive* (*Dem reech?* Did they arrive?)

arrow = *aro*

ask = *aaks (Patlish: hax)*

at = *a* (She's at work. = *Shi de a werk*.)

attend = *atten*; *goh* (*Mi goh St. Bess School*: I attend St. Bess School.)

avocado = *pear* (with this book's spelling: *pier*)

bag = *bag* (*wan bag a tings!* = an abundance of happenings or excitement)

bath = *baat* ("*Get a baat*" regionally refers to obeah folk rituals of using potions to "wash off" someone.)

bed = (furniture) bed; flowerbed, callaloo bed, etc.

belong = *bilang/billang* (*Dem billang to ar.* They belong to her. [Patlish: *bilanx*])

bike = (loanword) heavy roaring-motor two-wheeler (not usually bicycle)

birth = *brrt/birt*

biscuit = cookie or Amer. *biscuit* (American and British meaning)

blanket = *blang-kit*

boiled = *(bwaïl) bwyil*

bonus = *(buonos) bwonus; braata*

boy = *bwaai*; *likl bwaai* (little boy)

break = (v.) *brok;* broken = *brokop:* "*o*" is as in "son." Note: A break is a *briek*.

breakfast = *brekfass* (regionally: *brekfos, brekfaas*)

brother = *bredda*

business = *bizniz* (same pronunciation as English)

butter = *bota*

care = *kiah; kier* (*Dem noh get noh kier:* They get no care.)

careless = *kieh lis*

carry = *kiarry; kiar* (also: *kiari it = kiariit* [pronounced *kiareet*] "bring it; carry it")

cash = *kiash*

ceiling = *seelin (siilin)*

cellphone = *selfuon*

church = *church; tchutch (choch)*

class = *klaass*

clothes = *kluoz*

coconut = *kukkanat; kwoknat*

collect = *ka-lek*

come = *kom; kum* (regionally, you'll hear *"kum"* as in *"Kum Ba Ya"*)

computer = *komp-yuutah*

correct = *karrek*

cruel = *kruwil*

daily = *evry dieh; a dieh time; dielih*

daughter = *daata*

departure = *dipaacha*

designer = *diz I na*

diet = *da-yat*

digital = *dijji-tal (dijital)*

dollar = (*sing./pl.*) *dalla*

done = *dun* (sp. *don*, which rhymes with "fun")

doze = *dwuz; nap*

enter = *enta; kum een*

every = *evri* (homophone of English "ev'ry")

extinguisher = *extinguisha*

eye = *ai* (regionally: *yai*)

factory = *faktchrih*

fill = *full* (fill in: *filliin*, e.g. "fill it in" = *full it een/full it out*)

fitness = *fitniss*

forget = *figgat; figget* (*A dat mek mi figat/figet.* = That's what made me forget.)

forgive = *fi giv*

fuel = *fiuwil*

full-fledged = *fulflej*

gallivant = *gialivaant* (roam cavalierly)

ghost = *dopi; duppy* (Patlish: *gwoss*)

going = *gwyin; gwain*

grandfather = *granfaada; grampah*

grandmother = *granny (grani)*

handkerchief = *ang-krr-chiv; krrchiv*

hear = *ier*

heed = *iid (tek iid* = take heed)

help = *elp*

here = *ya; ya-soh*

how = *ou* (how much = *ummutch; omoch*)

hurt = *at (Patlish: ert)*

husk = *(verb) ux*; (noun) *usk*; (husky = *oski*)

impact = *impak*

important = *impuor-tant*

in = *een; inna*

inconstant = *"somtaiimish/sometime-ish"*: blow hot-and-cold

internet = *intannet (inta-net)*

iron = *I yan*

island = *I lan; I lant*

jeans = *jeenz/jiinz* (denim pants/jacket: *jeenz pants/jeenz jakit*)

karate = *karaati; karaachi*

keep = *kip* or *kiip*

leave = *lef*

let = *mek*

lettuce = *lettiss (letis)*

literature = *lichricha (litch ritcha)*

magazine = *maaga ziin*

make = *mek* (You make/made them into... = *Yu tek dem mek...*)

makeup = *mekkup; miekup*

medicine = *medisn*

meeting = *miitn (meetn)*

menu = (*men-yu*) *menu*

message = *messij*

money = *money* (English cognate)

must[1] = *mos* (*"Yu mos wiet."* You must wait.)

must[2] = *mosi* (*probably:* *"Dem mosi gaan."* They must've gone. They probably left.)

national = *nashinal*

no = *no, nuoh* (*noh/naa* means "not")

normal = *naamal*

not = *noh; naa* (I don't know why he's not leaving. *Mi noh nuoh wemek* im *naa lef.*)

now = *now* (regional: *nung; nong*)

object = *abjek*

other = *adda*

our = *ow-wa (oua)*

pee = *(v./n.) wiiwi* [pronounced *"wee-wi"*]

painter = *pienta*

paper = *pieppa*

phone = *fwun (fuon)*

picture = *pitcha* (In broken Patwa, you'll hear *pitch-ta.*)

pillow = *pilla*

plantain = *plantn*

plenty = *plenty*

porridge = *parrij*

printer = *printa*

probably = *prably; mussi* (*Dem mussi left:* They probably left. They must've gone.)

product = *prodok (proh-duck)*

protect = *pruttek; prittek*

put = *put* (put down = *puddung*)

quickly = *kwik-kwik*

race = *riess* (racism = *riessizzim*)

recommend = *rekkommen*

safety = *sieffty or si-yeffitty*

salad = *vejittebl; salad* (rural/regionally: *salad* = large tomato)

sandals = *slandaz; slippaz* (no singular for either)

shut = *shut*

speed limit = *speed limit* (loanword)

stand = *stanop*; a platform stand, etc.: *stan* (to take a stand: *fi tek a stan*)

stubborn = *stoban; aad yez*

support = *sopuot* (English phonics: "*sup woat*")

swimsuit = *baatsuut*

take = *tek*

talk = *taak*

tear = *rip, tear* (with this book's literal spelling: *tier*)

text = *tex*

these = *dem yah* (these things: *dem ting yah; dem sopm yah*)

those = *dem de* (those things: *dem ting de; dem sopm de*)

tired = *ta-yad (taïad)*

today = *(tude) to deh; tiddeh* (tomorrow = *tu marroh*)

touchy = *tut-chiz; tochiz*

unacceptable = *noh akseptebl* (Acceptable sounds the same in Patwa.)

usual = *(yuujal) yoojwal*; unusual = *an-yuujal*; usually = *yuujali*

victory = *viktchrih (viktri)*

vomit = *(n.) vamit; (v.) tchrouop*

wait = *wiet; wiet fa; wiet pan*

water = *waata*

what = *weh; wa*

when = *wen*

where = *weh (we)*

who = *(uu) oo*; whose = *oofa (uu-fa)*

why = *wai; wemmek; wammek (wemek)*

wire = *wa ya* (*wa-ya fenss* = chain-link fence)

work = *wok* ("*o*" as in "*son*") or in some contexts: *werk*

worth = *wert; (wot)wut*; worthless = *wutliss; wukliss)*

zipper = *zip*

Cognate Lists

Loanwords: These are but a few of the English words traditionally used in Patwa. Yet, please note: They might all be spelt differently with the new orthography's vowel patterns (e.g., *aktiviti, ad, agriiment, bluum, korant,* etc.). Still, other than using single consonants, where this list uses double, and adhering to the double vowels, you will find that this list has English words that are as near to Patwa words as you could ever imagine.

A – E: ability, absent, activity, add, admit, agreement, animal, antics, app, arrogant, assembly, assistant, bag, bank, bar; bed, bedroom, beg, belt, bet, bid, big, blank, blink, bloom; brag, bring, chat, check, chess, chips, clap, comment, compliment, count, crash, crisis, critical, cub, cud, cup, currant, current, cut, damp, dam, dejected, dependent, diagram, dignity, did, dig, dim, dip, disappear, discredit, disco, discount, discuss, dish, dissident, drag, edify, embassy, establishment, esteem, equality, event, express

F – N: fabric, fantastic, ferry, festival, fifteen, fifty, fin, finish, get, greedy, green, grip, immigrant, impediment, imply, India, inn, instant, instrument, jerk, jump, kangaroo, kayak, kingdom, kit, lab, lamp, latch, look, lunch, luscious, management, mango, map, medical, menu, mini, minibus, mood, moot, mount, much, nap, napkin, noon, noun

O – S: outfit, outlandish, outlet, pandemic, pants, pedigree, peel, penny, permanent, picnic, plan, plastic, plaza, plenty, press, print, productivity, proud; rabbit, reference, remedy, rental, rack, rich, sanitary, scout, scraps, screen, servant, shenanigans, sick, signal, sing, skinny, skip, skit, sleep, slip, son, spoon, stack, stamp, stash, statistics, step, steep, stick, street, stuck, stylish, subservient, subsidy, sun, sweet, swim, switch

T – Z: taxi, teddy, tell, territory, tip, turf, twenty, tyrant, unit, unity, university, urban, valid, validity, verb, visibility, watch, wax, well, willful, win, zebra, zed, zinc, zigzag (To romp or to move, in a zigzag pattern, on a bike, etc., is to *"dili dali"* in Patwa.)

Aural Cognates

The following words sound the same in Patwa but, unlike the traditional literal cognate list in which only vowels might differ, these aural cognates are spelt **very** differently:

A – D: absolute, accent, acceptable, account, achievement, acoustics, active, algebra, align, alignment, ambulance, analysis, analyze, appear, apply, arrive, arrival, assume, balance, bear, beautiful, belief, believe, beverage, biannual, bias, bib, Bible, bicycle

bike, bite, book, boot, bread, bumptious, business, busy, buy, byte, brush, bulk, bulky, bus, but, by, cent, chef, cheese, chemistry, chicken wing, chief, city, clean, climb, clout, club, colonel, combine, compete, completely, cotton, country, create, criteria, critic, criticize, critique, crucial, cruise, cue, cure, curfew, curriculum, cute, deaf, dear, decide, deep, deer, defeated, delicacy, dense, dent, derive, derogatory, detergent, deviant, device, devious, done, double, dress, drink, drive, drum, dynamic

E – M: each, earn, easy, emergency, enough, equal, exclude, exert, expensive, expert, far, feminine, fetch, few, file, fight, five, flourish, flu, food, frequent, fresh, fridge, fun, furnish, good, guidance, guitar, ice cream, idea, imaginary, immaculate, impeccable, impede, improve, include, intensity, intuitive, inquisitive, invisible, intelligent, jealous, jet-ski, journey, justice, justify, kitten, knife, language, lack, laugh, league, learn, level, life, light, like, lip, lose, love, lovable, loud, luggage, lyrics, machine, management, many, marine, marriage, masculine, maximum, media, merge, microchip, mighty, mimic, minute, monetize, money, move, movie, musical, musician, mystic

N – P: new, niece, night, nine, nourish, nurse, nutritious, obedient, peaceful, peanut, peas, perfume, pie, piece, plant, please, possessive, practicality, practice, preliminary, present, presentable, preside, president, presume, previous, price, pride, prime, prince, principle, productive, proficient, prove, pub, public, publish, pulp, puppy, puzzle

Q – S: quibble, quack, quad, qualify, quality, queen, quell, quick, quilt, quit, quiz, ramshackle, reach, ready, reason, reasonable, rebel, recipe, religious, renew, repeat, restaurant, result, return, rhyme, ride, rig, righteousness, rights, ripe, room, rubble, rum, rural, rustic, rumble, rusty, satisfy, school, scramble, scrounge, scrub, serve, service, side, sieve, sign, silent, simple, simplicity, skirt, sneak, snoop, soup, special, sprinkle, stigmatize, style, subsidize, subversive, success, surf, sweat, Sweden

T – Z: ten, ticket, tide, time, tongue, touch, tough, twelve, two, ultimate, uncle, value, valuable, vegetable, venue, verge, verse, vie, view, vigilant, visit, vital, vitality, vitamin, wean, wear, weave, welcome, weird, wide, wreak, young, zucchini

Braata

Aal a wi nuo Jomiekan pati, bot we yu nuo bout dieda fuud dem?
*(*We all know Jamaican patties, but what do you know about the other foods?)

Do you know these?

flitaz: flaked codfish fried in batter (Originally, it was called *stamp an' go*.)

banaana flitaz: mashed ripe bananas fried in batter (*Eng.* fritters)

dukunu: sweet cornmeal dessert boiled in banana leaf

mannish waata: goat-head soup

fish tea/fish tii: cups of fish soup with okra and diced veggies; a broth like savory tea

fish & bammy: escoveitch fish and a cassava side dish (also *festival*)

roast fish: *(ruos fish)* fish stuffed with herbs and vegetables, and grilled in foil

peppa swims: Scotch bonnet shrimp (goes well with *sky juice*)

fraï dumplin: Johnny cake made of fried dough

bulla & pear: small round cake & avocado (Most locals just say "pear.")

rundung/rondong: delicious coconut milk simmered with fish dishes

Immersion: *Pan di Luocal Menu* (On the Local Menu)

Dem sen kom kaal wi fi tiich dem fi kuk. Mek shuor dem kian pieh wi! They sent (and called) for us to teach them to cook. Make sure they can pay us!

Recipe: Escoveitch Fish & Bammy (*Eskovich Fish an Bami*)

Staat Wid di Snappa

1. *Rinss di fish weh dun skiel an guts* (*guts/gots* = fish guts removed).

2. *Seezn it wid saalt an peppa.*
3. *Giit a likl slash wid di naif kierful, soh it noh kerl up.*
4. *Res di fish inna di at-at aïl inna wan fryin pan.* (Put the fish very carefully in the hot oil in the frying pan.)

FYI: Fi a kwaata poun fish, kuk it bout sevn minit pan di tuu saïd til it kuk prapali. Mek it kuk kriss.

Translation: Starting with the Snapper

Rinse the scaled and gutted fish. Pat it dry, season it with salt and pepper, and score both sides of the fish so the fish doesn't "curl up" but fries evenly. Carefully lay the fish in hot oil in a sauté pan or "Dutchie" (kettle-shaped Jamaican open pot). For a quarter-pound fish, fry about seven minutes on each side until fully cooked ("properly"). Make it crispy.

Use some of the leftover oil to simmer strips of: onion/chuo-cho/pepper/carrots in a little vinegar with pimento for a few minutes, to garnish and top it off. This truly makes it Escoveitch. (FYI: "*chuo-cho*" is called "chayote" squash vegetable in Hispanic markets.)

Bammy
Ingreedient (Ingredients)

2 bammy

kuoknat aïl (coconut oil)

waata aar kuoknat milk (water or coconut milk)

Direkshan (Directions)

1. *Suok di bammy inna kukkanat milk aar waata, fi aaf owa ar soh.*
(Soak the bammy in coconut milk or water for thirty minutes or so.)

2. *At up di aïl inna wan fryin pan.*
Heat the oil in a sauté pan.

3. *Put iin di bammy kierful; noh akl it til it gwol.*
Put it in carefully; don't mess with it, until it fries golden.

4. *Tun it uova kierful.*
Carefully turn it over.

5. *Fraï di nex side lark ou you du di for saïd.*
Fry the other side of the bammy like you did the first side.

6. *Drien it pan a napkin.*
Drain it on a napkin.

7. *Niam di bammy wid yu Snappa fish aar eevn by itself!*
Eat the bammy with your snapper or even by itself!

Yu Dweet! You did it!

You made it to the finish line with style! We've come to the end of *Instant Patwa!*

Fram Biginnin to En
                        Henriques

Ka-lek yu sirfittikkit;

Yu riich di en.

Tek a likl briek,

Den riid di buk aggen!

A nof taim yu riid it?

Nuo prablem!

Praktis an iid it!

Waak gud, mi fren!

You know how to pronounce and translate that poem now (e.g., *riich*/reach; *buk*/book; *riid*/read; *taim*/time; *iid*/take heed of). You've come a long way!

May you enjoy your Patwa skills!

Da Patwa Sirfittikkit Ya

a fi:

_____(niem)

fi finish di Patwa klaas

_____, inna

20__

Kangratiulieshan! Yu don Instant Patwa!

References

1. The World Factbook (population statistics, as at July 2020)

2. United Nations (un.int) lists Jamaica's official language and size.

3. *Class, Codes and Control*, Basil Bernstein, 2003, Routledge and Kegan Paul, Ltd.

4. *The Rastafarians: Twentieth Anniversary Edition*, Leonard E. Barrett, Sr., 1997, Beacon Press

5. *Jamaica Talk: Three Hundred Years of the English Language in Jamaica*, Frederic Gomes Cassidy, 1961, Univ. Press of the West Indies

Recommended Resources

Language, Race and the Global Jamaican, First Edition, 2020, Palgrave MacMillan, Dr. Hubert Devonish and Dr. Karen Carpenter

My Mother Who Fathered Me: A Study of the Families in Three Selected Communities of Jamaica, Edith Clarke, 2002, University Press of the West Indies; 3rd Edition (1st 1957)

Miss Lou: Louise Bennett and the Jamaican Culture, by Jamaica's Poet Laureate Professor Mervyn Morris, Randle Publishing, 2014 (Be aware of anglicized spelling in some poetry, but Miss Lou's use of idiom is lovely.)

YouTube uploads by "Jamaicanlanguageunit" are great and feature Maroons speaking Kromanti, related to the Akan Twi. It also features *"Raitin Jamiekan di Jamiekan Wie"* (Writing Jamaican the Jamaican Way).

Wake the Town and Tell the People: Dancehall Culture in Jamaica, Duke University Press Books, 2000, Norman Stolzoff

Memba fi lisn foundieshan miuuzik: Remember to listen to "foundation" music from The Mighty Diamonds, Dennis Brown; Culture; Joseph Cotton; Wailers; etc. In Dancehall, Pinchers is the most amazing teacher of Patwa with songs such as *"Chuu Mi De De"*/"Because I Was There" and *"Si Mi Ya"*/"Here I Am."

Get to Know the Author

I love languages, especially standard English and pure Patwa. This love is what has inspired *Instant Patwa: Speak and Understand Jamaican Patwa.* I can hardly wait for visitors and expatriates to dive into this book and learn the language locals and tourists love.

I also have a heart for the plight of the bilingual people of the English-speaking Caribbean and any other Commonwealth people whose first language is Creole/Patwa. Many such urban students' mastery of English has been hampered not only by the lack of ESL support but also by the misconception that they are a monolingual people with broken English. You can see how the lack and the misconception reinforce and perpetuate each other. The less than stellar scores in GCE and CXC English Language exams have, for too long, been seen as a failure of the student and not the process. Creole speakers will find this book very useful in filling the process gaps, and that's another reason this book has been my labor of love.

I write an eclectic variety of books including novels on vast topics. Visit henriquespublishing.com to find more books to enjoy! One love!

— Henriques

Jamaican Patwa Is Fun!

Jamaica's unofficial language adds to her popularity and mystique – but it can baffle fans of Patwa. Achieving fluency in Jamaican Patwa requires a strategic approach that shows why and where what we hear seems to run together.

Instant Patwa brings you that demystifying approach.

English speakers are understood in Jamaica. Tourists will find that locals understand English, though most locals do not speak fluent English. However, if you know only English without a grasp of the day-to-day language, you're likely to understand the local people way less than they understand you.

The desired dynamic is equal understanding. With this in mind, *Instant Patwa* is written with a focus on what you'll hear (how native speakers speak), to show you how we say what we say. That's how *Instant Patwa* hones your listening skills and helps you to master spoken Patwa very quickly.

Jamaican Patwa is relatively simple -- when you've learnt its secret patterns. After learning those patterns in this book, you should have a great grasp of Patwa. Just as important: After reading this book, the Jamaican students who struggle with standard English will find the official language far more accessible.

If you're an expatriate in Jamaica, *Instant Patwa* gives you an edge. If you're a non-native creative writer, songwriter, or artiste in any genre of musical arts and theatre/entertainment (film, etc.), you've now got a great grasp of authentic Patwa in your toolkit to create real Jamaican lyrics or characters/dialogue. If you're purely a fan of Jamaican Patwa anywhere in the world, what a great party skill you'll have after reading this book!

www.ingramcontent.com/pod-product-compliance
Lightning Source LLC
Chambersburg PA
CBHW051132160426
43195CB00014B/2440